CO

ENGLISH GUIDES
9:LINKING WORDS

Sylvia Chalker

THE UNIVERSITY OF BIRMINGHAM

COLLINS COBUILD

HarperCollins*Publishers*

HarperCollins Publishers
77-85 Fulham Palace Road
London W6 8JB

COBUILD is a trademark of William Collins Sons & Co Ltd

First Published 1996

2 4 6 8 10 9 7 5 3 1

ISBN 0 00 375047 7

Corpus Acknowledgements

We would like to acknowledge the assistance of the many hundreds of individuals and companies who have kindly given permission for copyright material to be used in The Bank of English. The written sources include many national and regional newspapers in Britain and overseas; magazine and periodical publishers; and book publishers in Britain, the United States, and Australia. Extensive spoken data has been provided by radio and television broadcasting companies; research workers at many universities and other institutions; and numerous individual contributors. We are grateful to them all.

Note

The author and publisher are grateful to the following for permission to reproduce the following:
page 199, BBC Midlands Radio; John Taynton show, 17.02.92
page 196, 'Close encounters and conspiracy of silence' by Robert Matthews, published 20 August 1995 in The Daily Telegraph, © The Telegraph plc, London, 1995.
page 198, 'War crimes novelist has fantasy life' by Geoffrey Lee Martin, published 23 August 1995 in The Daily Telegraph, © The Telegraph plc, London, 1995.

Computer typeset by Tradespools Ltd, Frome, Somerset.

Printed and bound in Great Britain by
Caledonian International Book Manufacturing Ltd, Glasgow, G64.

Contents

Foreword

The *Guide to Linking Words* is one of a series of COBUILD ENGLISH GUIDES to particular areas of difficulty for learners of English.

The author, Sylvia Chalker, is one of Britain's foremost writers on English grammar, and we are particularly pleased that she accepted our invitation to write this *Guide* for us.

It is important to remember that language does not consist simply of isolated remarks and statements; in both written and spoken language, learners need to be able to recognize and use the various techniques for linking sentences and clauses together into longer utterances, and relating them to a wider context. We hope that this *Guide* will enable them to deal confidently with this key aspect of the language, which has been relatively neglected by traditional grammar books.

This book, like all COBUILD books, is derived from studying the evidence in The Bank of English, a massive corpus of language now containing over 250 million words. The examples are taken directly from the corpus, and the frequency of words affects the prominence given to them here. The emphasis on real language ensures that the learner is able to observe the linking strategies used by actual native speakers of English, and can then go on to apply them, in a natural and convincing way, in his or her own writing and conversation.

We hope that you find this book helpful and easy to use. Please write to us with any comments or suggestions about how to improve COBUILD publications. We have set up an e-mail address (editors@cobuild.collins.co.uk) to make it easier for users to correspond with us. You can write to us at the following address:

COBUILD
University of Birmingham Research Park
Vincent Drive
Birmingham B15 2SQ

The COBUILD Series

Founding Editor-in-Chief John Sinclair

Editorial Director Gwyneth Fox

Editorial Team

Editors	Jane Bradbury John Williams	*Computer Staff*	Jeremy Clear Tim Lane
Editorial Assistance	Alice Grandison Sean Lynch David Morrow	*Secretarial Staff*	Sue Crawley Michelle Devereux

Acknowledgements: We would like to thank Gill Francis, Martin Hewings, Susan Hunston, Elizabeth Manning, and Debbie Seymour for their help at various stages in the production of this *Guide*.

Introduction

Sometimes you can write or say what you want to express in a single simple sentence. But many utterances, whether written or spoken, consist of longer stretches of language.

Linking Words deals with the words and phrases that link one sentence or one clause with another, showing the connections. The term 'linking word' (or 'linking adverb') is sometimes narrowly used to mean what we here call connectors. This *Guide* takes a wider view and looks at other 'referring' words and other 'linking' devices.

Chapter 1 explains the differences between two important kinds of linking words – conjunctions and connectors.

Chapter 2 concentrates on conjunctions – particularly co-ordinating conjunctions and adverbial conjunctions. It also deals with connectors that have similar meanings.

Chapter 3 deals with more connectors, but ones that do not have corresponding conjunctions.

Chapter 4 describes the links that join relative clauses and noun clauses to their sentences. It also looks at how non-finite and verbless clauses are linked to their sentences, often without any linking word.

Chapter 5 looks at the role of pronouns, determiners, and some other words insofar as they refer to and substitute for other items in written and spoken language.

Chapter 6 looks at the way nouns are used to refer to other nouns (or noun groups) or to longer pieces of text.

Chapter 7 concentrates on some informal linking words that are particularly used in conversation.

Chapter 8 deals with an important set of adverbs – sentence adjuncts – which grammatically speaking are not linking words at all. They are included here for two reasons. Firstly, in some grammar books they are lumped with connectors as 'sentence adverbs' because, like connectors, they serve as a sort of comment on a whole sentence, rather than being a part of it. But their function and usage is different from that of connectors, and the two types of adverb need to be distinguished. So, secondly, like the strictly linking words described in earlier chapters they act as markers to help the listener or reader follow the discourse more easily.

A set of exercises follows, some consisting of short examples, others of longer pieces of text. All the exercises are based on the linking words and functions discussed in the previous chapters, and can be used in the classroom to reinforce and test students' knowledge of this key area of language. An Answer Key is also included, making the exercises ideal for self-study.

It is important to realize that many English words and phrases have more than one meaning and more than one grammatical use. This *Guide* concentrates on linking functions, but many of the words and phrases described can be used in other ways.

Sylvia Chalker
London 1996

Glossary of grammatical terms

The following Glossary gives brief definitions of some of the most important grammatical terms used in this *Guide*. Many of the terms are defined and discussed in more detail in the main text. Precise references can be found in the Index.

absolute clause a non-finite or verbless clause that contains its own subject, e.g. *weather permitting.*

adverb clause a clause that functions in a sentence in much the same way as a single adverb does, e.g. *I'll come as soon as I can.*

adverbial a word or group of words (including single adverbs) that functions like an adverb.

apposition the placing of a noun group or noun clause after another noun, with both parts referring to the same person or thing, e.g. *There was a danger / that they would decide to leave.*

complement a word, word group, or clause that 'completes' the verb (particularly a link verb such as 'seem' or 'be'), e.g. *You seem upset... The fact is I can't afford it.*

complex sentence a sentence that consists of a main clause and at least one subordinate clause, e.g. *I didn't buy it, although I liked it.*

compound-complex sentence a sentence that consists of two or more main clauses, together with at least one subordinate clause, e.g. *I put my arm around him and steered him to the sofa, where he collapsed.*

compound sentence a sentence that consists of two or more main clauses linked by a co-ordinating conjunction, e.g. *They picked her up and took her into the house.*

concession the idea of contrast, as expressed by particular conjunctions, connectors, and types of subordinate clause.

conjunct another word for 'connector'.

conjunction a word that links together two clauses, phrases, or words. There are two types of conjunction – co-ordinating conjunctions and subordinating conjunctions.

connector an adverb or other adverbial that can link two separate sentences, e.g. *I can't do anything just now. It won't matter a lot, though.*

content disjunct a sentence adjunct that shows your attitude to what you are describing, e.g. *Fortunately, the weather that winter was reasonably mild*, or your opinion as to its likelihood, e.g. *Perhaps they might help him.*

co-ordinated clauses two clauses linked by a co-ordinating conjunction, e.g. *This is really confidential and I've not told it to anyone.*

co-ordinating conjunction a word such as 'and', 'but', or 'or' which joins two clauses, phrases, or words of the same grammatical type.

co-ordinating pair a co-ordinating conjunction that consists of two words or phrases separated from each other in the sentence. The main co-ordinating pairs are 'both...and', 'either...or', 'not only...but also', and 'neither...nor'.

co-ordinator another term for 'co-ordinating conjunction'.

correlatives another term for 'co-ordinating pairs'.

defining relative clause a relative clause that identifies the person or thing being talked about, e.g. *The office that had been cleared for them was austere but functional.*

demonstrative one of the words 'this', 'that', 'these', and 'those', used in front of a noun, e.g. *this woman*, or as a pronoun, e.g. *That looks nice.*

determiner one of a group of words, including 'the', 'a', 'some', and 'my', which are used at the beginning of a noun group.

discourse marker a word or phrase in spoken language that signals to the listener how he or she should understand what is being said, e.g. *Now look here, you're wrong.*

disjunct another term for 'sentence adjunct'.

ellipsis the leaving out of words when they are 'recoverable' from elsewhere in the context, e.g. *Come if you can* shows ellipsis of a second 'come'.

fluency filler a word or sound in spoken English which has no particular meaning, but which makes the speaker sound more fluent, e.g. *Well I mean you see the Scots are very proud of their country.*

'-ing'-clause a clause-like structure in which the verb occurs in the present participle without a finite auxiliary verb, e.g. *It was certainly the best meal I had had since leaving home.*

nominal clause another term for 'noun clause'.

nominal relative clause a type of 'wh'-clause, often one that does not represent a question, in which the 'wh'-word has a double function, standing for something in the main clause and as a relative pronoun in the relative clause, e.g. *What you need is a change of scene*, where 'what' roughly means 'that which'.

non-defining relative clause a relative clause which gives more information about someone or something, but which is not needed to identify them, e.g. *Paul's father, with whom he had had a close relationship, died suddenly.*

non-finite clause a clause-like structure containing a verb that is not a finite verb, e.g. *Water is liquid, but when heated it becomes vapour.*

noun clause a 'that'-clause or 'wh'-clause that has the same function in a sentence as a noun or noun group.

pro-form a general word or phrase, such as 'here', 'there', 'now', and 'then', which can be used to replace a more specific word or phrase, in the same kind of way as a pronoun replaces a noun.

quantity pronoun a pronoun such as 'both' or 'many' which allows you to refer to a quantity of something, often without being precise about the exact amount or number.

reduced clause a subordinate structure which does not contain a finite verb, but from which a finite verb can be understood, e.g. *She wanted to sleep if possible.*

reduced relative clause a structure which has the same function as a relative clause, but which has no subject or finite verb, e.g. *He took out a folder containing my proposal*, where 'containing' is equivalent to 'that contained'.

sentence adjunct an adverb or other adverbial that shows your attitude to what you are saying (the contents), e.g. *Personally, I think you'd be better off here in the States*, or explains how you are speaking (your style), e.g. *We're getting a little tired of it, frankly.*

sentence adverb See **8.2**.

stative verb a verb such as 'be', 'seem', or 'know', which describes a state rather than an action, and is not normally used in a continuous tense.

style disjunct a sentence adjunct that explains how you are speaking, e.g. *Quite honestly, I don't know if it was worth it.*

subject-auxiliary inversion the placing of the auxiliary verb before the subject of a sentence, required, for example, after some negative expressions, e.g. *Not only did they win, but they also changed the nature of their team.*

subordinate clause a clause which cannot be a complete sentence on its own, and is dependent on another clause. Subordinate clauses include adverb clauses, noun clauses, relative clauses, and also non-finite and verbless clauses.

subordinating conjunction a conjunction that begins a subordinate clause.

subordinator another term for 'subordinating conjunction'.

substitution the use of words – particularly pronouns, the verb 'do', and 'so' and 'not' standing for a predicate – instead of repeating the original words, e.g. *I asked him to telephone me, but he failed to do so.* (Notice how this differs from ellipsis, where words are simply omitted, e.g. *...but he failed to.)*

'that'-clause a clause starting with the conjunction 'that', or no conjunction at all, for example a clause which is used to report what someone has said, e.g. *She said that she'd wash up for me... She said she'd wash up for me.*

'to'-infinitive clause a non-finite clause in which the verb occurs in its base form, preceded by 'to', e.g. *To do this, you need to be firm and assertive... For the attack to succeed, surprise was essential.*

verbless clause a clause-like structure which does not contain a verb, but from which a verb can be understood, e.g. *She wanted to sleep if possible.*

'wh'-clause a clause starting with a 'wh'-word, often a subordinate clause reporting a question, e.g. *She asked what I'd brought with me.*

A note on typography

In the main text of this *Guide*, lexical items (words and phrases) are shown in **bold type** at their first or most important mentions; 'quotation marks' are used for subsequent or incidental mentions. Technical terms in grammar are shown in ***bold italic*** at their first or most important mentions; many of these terms are defined in the above Glossary.

Slashes or parentheses may be used to show alternative forms of phrases, e.g. 'generally/broadly/roughly speaking' stands for the three phrases 'generally speaking', 'broadly speaking', and 'roughly speaking', while 'without (any) doubt' means both 'without doubt' and 'without any doubt'.

Examples are shown in *italic*, with the word or phrase under discussion underlined. Where an example is used to illustrate a grammatically incorrect formulation, this is indicated by the symbol ✗. A contrasting 'correct' example is indicated by the symbol ✓.

1 Conjunctions and connectors: outline

Grammatical ways of joining clauses

1.1 When you want to write or say something which is too complicated to express in a simple sentence (a sentence with only one finite verb), you can of course write separate sentences. There are also two straightforward ways of joining sentences together:

- You can link sentences together using a ***co-ordinating conjunction*** such as 'and'. The original sentences are now clauses of equal importance (***co-ordinated clauses***) and the sentence is a ***compound sentence***.

  This is really confidential and I've not told it to anyone.

- You can keep your original sentence as the main clause of the new sentence, and add a ***subordinate*** (i.e. less important) ***clause***, using a ***subordinating conjunction***, such as 'when'. Your new sentence is now a ***complex sentence***.

  We also tend to trust people more when they look at us directly.
  (main clause followed by subordinate clause)

1.2 More than two clauses can be joined in one sentence, using either of these methods or a mixture of both. With a mixture of co-ordinate and subordinate clauses, your new sentence is now a ***compound-complex sentence***.

I put my arm across his shoulders and steered him to the sofa, where he collapsed. (main, main, subordinate)

He had always loved Clara and he had always hoped that he could make her love him. (main, main, subordinate)

It was still early, and although she was fatigued her mind was restless. (main, subordinate, main)

He had always written like that, although when he was small Sofia had taught him to write 'D' the proper way. (main, subordinate, subordinate)

1.3 Another, looser, way of showing a connection between two clauses, and particularly between separate sentences, is to use a rather special type of adverb called a ***connector*** (sometimes also called a ***conjunct*** or a ***linking adjunct***). Some examples of connectors are 'moreover', 'nevertheless', and 'otherwise'.

Conjunctions and connectors: grammatical differences

1.4 Conjunctions and connectors share many of the same meanings, and some words, such as 'before', 'though', and 'however', function as both. But the grammar of these two kinds of linking word is different in various ways (**1.5–1.10**).

1.5 A ***conjunction*** normally combines two (or more) clauses into one sentence, often with a comma separating them, but sometimes with no punctuation mark.

Before you decide to be a soldier, you have got to read these books.

Ms Johnson was looking very embarrassed, though she was smiling.

This was a selling job, however you look at it.

A ***connector***, by contrast, often shows a connection between two separate sentences, so there is a full stop at the end of the first sentence.

Now he's more focused on his work. Before, he was distracted, always making plans to go out.

'I can't do anything for several days,' he said. 'It won't matter a lot, though'.

There was no longer any abdominal pain. However, the patient experienced low back pain and cramps in the legs.

Of course, you have some choice with punctuation, but a comma is not usually strong enough between two clauses which are linked by a connector.

1.6 A ***connector*** has a rather 'detached' role in its clause. So it is often separated by a comma or commas from the rest of its clause.

Before, I had oysters for breakfast and now I've changed them for porridge.

However, the patient experienced low back pain.

A ***conjunction*** belongs to its clause, so it is not normally separated from it by punctuation.

Before you decide to be a soldier…

1.7 Clauses that are introduced by a ***subordinating conjunction*** are grammatically incomplete without the rest of the sentence.

✗ *Before you decide to be a soldier.*

✗ *Though she was smiling.*

Clauses (or sentences) containing a ***connector*** certainly refer back to an earlier sentence, but are more grammatically complete.

✓ *Before, it would have been impossible.*
✓ *It won't matter a lot, though.*

1.8 Most ***conjunctions*** come at the beginning of their clause. ***Connectors*** are also usually at the beginning, but many can come later (and some, e.g. 'though' as a connector, must).

I have read and enjoyed the article you sent me. I do feel that several paragraphs are somewhat distorted, however.

1.9 Most clauses introduced by a ***conjunction*** can precede their main clause. The exceptions include 'so that' result clauses, and of course the second of two co-ordinated clauses. But a sentence containing a ***connector*** refers back to the preceding sentence. So a connector cannot appear in the first of two linked sentences, because it cannot refer forwards.

✗ *I do feel that several paragraphs are somewhat distorted, however. I have read and enjoyed the article you sent me.*

1.10 With the important exception of co-ordinators such as 'and', 'but', and 'or' (which can join single words), a ***conjunction*** usually introduces a finite clause, complete with subject and finite verb, although some conjunctions can also introduce a ***reduced clause***.

Hodge is disappointed, but philosophical about the decision. (...but he is philosophical...)

Although certain I had not actually broken a rib or two, I knew that something had gone wrong. (Although I was certain...)

If possible, choose a restaurant in advance. (If it is possible...)

A ***connector***, by contrast, does not grammatically belong so closely to a clause. It is there to indicate the speaker's or writer's assessment of how some second utterance relates to the preceding clause or sentence. Therefore the second utterance cannot be 'reduced' to a connector followed by a phrase or single word.

✗ *Hodge is disappointed, nevertheless philosophical about today's decision.*

Co-ordinating conjunctions: grammar and meaning

1.11 The main co-ordinating conjunctions are **and**, **but**, and **or**.

And is the most general conjunction in meaning. It is sometimes used simply to add one statement to another, where there is some connection of meaning.

The vehicle was muddy and the carpet inside needed sweeping.

You can also use **and** to add a statement where one event follows another in time, or as a result.

She caught Mark's arm and pulled him to his feet.

Russia spans 11 time zones and desperately needs satellites for a communications network good enough to attract Western investors.

I think you're a great family and I'm glad I'm going to join you.

Or usually suggests an alternative. There is also the more emphatic expression **or else**.

The new rules may not always be properly tested or they may simply be ignored.

The smell wasn't so bad in here, or else he was getting used to it.

But introduces a contrast, something surprising.

He went to his study, but he couldn't work.

Dean faced a similar charge but it was withdrawn.

Co-ordinating pairs

1.12 There are also several co-ordinating conjunctions which consist of pairs of words. These are known as ***co-ordinating pairs*** (or sometimes ***correlatives***). The first word adds emphasis to the meaning of the second.

The main co-ordinating pairs are:

both...and
either...or
not only...but (also)
neither...nor

When used to link two clauses together, **both...and** stresses that each of two facts is true or possible. **Either...or** joins alternatives. **Not only...but (also)** gives emphasis to two related facts, but particularly to the second. Sometimes these are surprising facts, the second even more surprising than the first. **Neither...nor** connects two negatives.

1.13 Like the main co-ordinating conjunctions, co-ordinating pairs normally join words or phrases of the same grammatical type. 'Either…or' and 'not only…but (also)' can join whole clauses, complete with their own subjects and verbs. If 'not only' comes at the beginning of a sentence, it requires subject-auxiliary inversion (if necessary using the verb 'do'). However, it can also come before the main verb of its clause without inversion.

Either you're lying or he must be an absolute wimp.

Not only did they win, but they also changed the nature of their team.

They not only printed my letter but they paid me £5.

(Note: some people would consider the third example here to be wrong, as the two items joined by 'not only…but' are not of the same grammatical type – 'printed my letter' is a verb plus an object, whereas 'they paid me £5' is a whole clause. The sentence would be grammatically correct if the second 'they' were omitted – 'They not only printed my letter but paid me £5'; 'printed my letter' and 'paid me £5' both consist of a verb plus an object.)

1.14 Here are some more examples of co-ordinating pairs:

Most of our flights have either taken off or landed by 11.30pm.

They either ignored the situation or treated it lightheartedly.

The National Bank was a place where women were either secretaries or oddities.

The claims were not only quite false but also very nearly dishonest.

This will benefit not only the employers but also the workers.

He both loved it and hated it.

Most unconfident people will have experienced their fair share of punishment both from others and from themselves.

Coeducation suits both boys and girls.

My client wants neither to buy nor to rent this flat.

I told them that neither the kidnappers nor my wife had turned up at the appointed time.

He dared show neither pleasure nor pain.

'Nor', 'neither', and 'either' as connectors

1.15 **Nor** and **neither** can also be used singly after a negative clause to introduce another negative clause. The first negative clause may contain a true negative word such as 'not' or 'never', or a broad negative such as 'hardly'. Subject-auxiliary inversion is needed after 'nor' and 'neither', and there is usually ellipsis in the verb group. 'Nor' and 'neither' may be preceded by a conjunction.

She didn't want anyone to know, and neither did I.

He wouldn't want the trouble. And nor would I.

She appeared not to recognize me. And nor did I desire it.

He could hardly look at it, nor examine it in my presence. (...nor could he examine...)

Alternatively, the second negative clause can contain a negative word plus a final **either**.

He never had any failures, but he never had any great successes either.

'I haven't really got anything planned. Are you doing anything?'— 'No, I haven't got anything planned either.'

Co-ordinating and subordinating conjunctions compared

1.16 A number of conjunctions are partly like co-ordinating conjunctions and partly like subordinating conjunctions. They are **yet** (in the sense of 'but'); **for** (in the sense of 'because'); **so** (in the sense of 'as a result'); and **then** (when it is used with the meaning of either 'next' or 'therefore').

There are several grammatical ways in which ***co-ordinating*** and ***subordinating conjunctions*** are different. These are explained in paragraphs **1.17–1.21**.

1.17 The ***co-ordinators*** 'and' and 'or' can link more than two clauses, and all but the final 'and' or 'or' can be omitted.

He grabbed my purse, opened it and stuffed it full.

You can pay cash, send a cheque, or use your credit card.

These are exceptions, however. Other conjunctions, including 'but', cannot semantically join more than two clauses. In the following sentence we understand 'and', not 'but', between the first two clauses:

He failed, got into debt, but then found a job in Brussels.

'And', 'or', and 'but' can also link two subordinate clauses to each other.

His wife had insulted him constantly at restaurants, because he ate too much bread and always finished off the meal with a rich pastry. (...and because he always finished off...)

In the letter Annie said she was sorry to have run off without a word, but that she was happy with her marriage and work. (...but said that she was happy...)

Tennison could recognize an emergency when he saw, or as in this case heard one. (...when he heard one.)

1.18 In clauses that are linked by 'and', 'or', or 'but', a shared subject is not always repeated.

He went up and found the bed hadn't been slept in.

I'd have been happy to attend the game, but have been advised by others not to.

As time went on he lapsed into long silences or became offensively off-hand.

Shared auxiliary verbs may also be omitted.

You should write to them or give them a ring some time. (...or you should give them...)

When two negative clauses in an 'and' relationship share the same subject, the second negative (and any shared auxiliaries) can be omitted. The two clauses are then joined by **or**.

He didn't keep them or have them printed. (i.e. He didn't keep them and he didn't have them printed.)

Shared subjects are also sometimes omitted after 'yet', 'so' (in the senses mentioned in paragraph **1.16**), and 'then' (in the sense of 'next').

There was a connection that I did not understand, yet felt.

Iron absorption has been extensively studied yet is still poorly understood.

I tried for the prison service and was turned down and so went to the jobcentre.

For a little while she waited, then went out herself.

He sighed, then continued.

Shared subjects and other words cannot be omitted from a 'for'-clause, nor from a ***subordinate clause***.

✗ *I bought it, for liked it.*
✗ *I didn't buy it, although liked it.*

1.19 The ***co-ordinators*** 'and', 'or', 'but', 'yet', and co-ordinating pairs, can join phrases or single words. This contrasts with most ***subordinating conjunctions***, which introduce clauses.

You should be able to divide the housework, shopping and cooking between you.

It's difficult but worthwhile.

Then add raisins, nuts, or little pieces of chocolate.

We're expecting to go back to London later today, or maybe on the first shuttle tomorrow.

Quiet, utterly genial, yet dignified, this gentleman struck me as a perfect example of 'a good citizen'.

Most of them are either dead or out of the country.

1.20 Clauses introduced by ***co-ordinators*** must usually follow the other clause they relate to, as in the examples above. For example, we cannot change:

He didn't want to be seen, so he carefully sauntered off in the opposite direction.

to:

✗ *So he carefully sauntered off in the opposite direction, he didn't want to be seen.*

'Then' (in the sense of 'therefore') can introduce a main clause following an 'if'-clause.

If he says he's got evidence, then he's got it.

But the order of the two clauses cannot be reversed.

✗ *Then he's got it, if he says he's got evidence.*

By contrast, many ***subordinate clauses*** can precede their main clause.

Because it is electric, there are no polluting exhaust gases.

Before the boys could answer, an angry voice was heard outside.

After they had played two sets, they went into the clubhouse and had lunch.

This 'only-as-a-second-clause' rule for co-ordinators seems so logical that some people consider any sentence beginning with 'and', 'but', or 'or' to be ungrammatical. However, if the new sentence refers back, like a second clause, to the previous sentence, this is acceptable.

You don't do a lot of checking in this particular job, unless you've been specially asked to. And in this case nobody was.

This wine will develop in a few more years. But it's excellent stuff right now.

Nobody took any notice of his opinions. Yet he remained proud and confident.

1.21 The ***co-ordinators*** 'and', 'or, 'but', and 'for' cannot be preceded by another conjunction. By contrast, 'yet', 'so', and ***subordinating conjunctions*** can be preceded by 'and', 'but', or 'or'.

I was sure he was telling the truth and yet I did find it hard to believe.

They could not see the river and so they did not know which way to run.

I do go out at night but only if I can use the car or if I'm not on my own.

Subordinate clauses: outline

1.22 There are three main types of ***subordinate clause***, based on the different functions they have in a sentence:

- ***adverb clauses*** – These play the same sort of role that single adverbs do. They are usually linked to the rest of the sentence by a subordinating conjunction.

- ***relative clauses*** – These are usually introduced by a relative pronoun. Their role is often adjectival (and they are occasionally described as adjective clauses.)

- ***noun clauses*** – These can be further subdivided into 'that'-clauses and 'wh'-clauses, usually linked to the sentence by 'that' or a 'wh'-word. Both types are referred to here as noun clauses, because their function is often similar to that of a noun. For example, they can be subjects or objects of a verb.

Most conjunctions and other linking subordinators are single words (e.g. 'although', 'because', 'if', 'who', 'that'), but some consist of two or more words (e.g. 'in case', 'as long as', 'on condition that').

2 Adverbial conjunctions plus related connectors

Adverb clauses

2.1 ***Adverb clauses*** function in sentences in much the same way as single adverbs do. Compare the following examples:

I'll come tomorrow. (time adverb)

I'll come as soon as I can. (time clause)

Subordinating adverbial conjunctions are very numerous. They introduce clauses concerned with meanings of time, condition, concession, contrast, purpose, reason, result, place, manner, and others.

Some of these same meanings are also shown by connectors. Adverbial conjunctions have therefore been grouped in this chapter with connectors, where appropriate, to show shared meanings and grammatical differences.

2.2 Some conjunctions can be followed by a reduced clause. These may be non-finite:

While waiting for the water to boil he made another trip to the bedroom.

'I had to copy the patterns by hand,' she says, 'and had no idea how they would look when finished.

or verbless:

She wanted to sleep if possible.

All connectors, by contrast, normally need to have a complete clause or sentence.

Time: conjunctions

2.3 ***Time clauses*** relate the time of the main clause to some other event or period. The relationship is usually clear from the conjunction used, and tense usage follows normal rules. Notice that when the main clause refers to the future only a present tense is needed in the time clause, because it acts as a 'background', not as a prediction. The same rule applies in conditional clauses.

The event or state in the main clause may be earlier than the time of the time clause:

Everything is carefully cleaned before it is passed on to you.

or later:

Zoe's confidence was shattered for a few months after her bag was snatched.

or at the same time:

He could have come while I was getting a coffee.

when

2.4 Tenses are particularly important with the very general conjunction **when**. With two simple past tense actions, the 'when'-clause action happened first.

When Tweed arrived, he was shown into Fairweather's office.

When they took the baby from me to clean her up, she let out a couple of good screams.

(Note: the co-ordinating conjunction 'and' sometimes relates two events in sequence, so if we want to make both events equally important we could say, for example, 'Tweed arrived and was shown into Fairweather's office.')

A ***stative verb*** in the 'when'-clause suggests a state already in existence, a sort of 'background' to the main-clause action.

She died when we were quite young.

He only drank when he was sure of being alone.

A past perfect tense in the 'when'-clause emphasizes that the first action was completed before the second.

When he had finished, he turned out the light.

When he had read this and risen to his feet he saw all the bystanders around him smiling.

If the 'when'-clause refers to the future, a present or present perfect tense (not 'will') is used.

I'll try to explain when I see you.

What will you do when you go back?

When you have finished, you will be shown to your bedroom.

When you have solved this mystery will you return to England?

2.5 With other tense combinations, the 'when'-clause can indicate the second or later event, often one which interrupts the earlier event.

When the phone rang, he was making himself a cheese sandwich.

We were driving around outside when unfortunately three old ladies emerged from the hotel and came straight across in front of us.

We had just gone to bed when we were startled by a forceful knocking at the door.

2.6 Instead of the conjunction 'when' (plus an adverbial clause) you can sometimes use a phrase such as 'on the day', 'at the moment', or 'the first time', followed by a relative 'that'-clause.

So do you ever go to the college of an evening on the days that you're working?

This came on the day I got my last bank statement.

He arrived at the very moment that the Civil Service was preparing radical administrative changes.

At the very moment my husband proposed to me, I said, 'Yes, I'll marry you'.

The first time I came here, I had the best night's sleep for months.

Similarly, a relative 'when'-clause following a noun such as 'day' or 'moment' can be used. (See **4.10**.)

Matty enjoyed talking to Mr Halloran, whom he met on the days when the greengrocer brought his van around.

There was a wave of dissatisfaction with President Bush's economic policy at the very moment when that policy was starting to come right.

Of course, if you do not need to specify the time so exactly, you can simply use an adverbial 'when'-clause.

Do you ever go to the college of an evening when you're working?

...whom he met when the greengrocer brought his van around.

after

2.7 **After** indicates that the event or state of the main clause is later than the event or state in the subordinate time clause. The use of tenses is very similar to the pattern in 'when'-clauses.

After Don told me this, he spoke of his mother.

He reached here right after we did.

After Dena had gone to bed he studied the picture again as he drank a brandy.

Laura went for a ride on her moped after Ian had left for work.

They were doing it long before we got here. And they'll be doing it long after we leave.

A letter will be sent to your family doctor as soon as possible after you have left hospital.

since

2.8 Since indicates the starting point in the past for a state or series of events which still continues now, or continues from some point in the past until a later time in the past. The 'since'-clause usually needs a past tense. You use a perfect tense in the main clause. **Ever since** is used for emphasis.

These drugs have been the mainstay of medical treatment since they first became available in 1950.

Things have improved since the inspector wrote his report.

He's been there ever since you left.

A lot had happened since they last met.

The family had lived in the Manor House since it had been built in 1573.

Note that, with 'since', it is usually wrong to use a present tense or simple past tense in the main clause.

✗ *He is there since you left.*
✗ *The family lived in the Manor House since it had been built in 1573.*

However, the simple present tense or simple past tense of the verb 'be' is normal in sentences of the following kind, where the emphasis is on the amount of time which has passed:

It is over ten years since we left college.

It's ten days since the accident happened.

It was forty years since Ingrid had first arrived in California.

before, until, till

2.9 Both **before** and **until** indicate that the event or state in the main clause is earlier in time than the one in the time clause. But 'until' stresses the stopping-point or the goal of the main-clause event or state.

Mr Major spoke to Mr Kohl shortly before the Chancellor flew to India.

I was already an old person before I stopped acting in that way.

They had known each other for only three months before he left Brisbane.

Read the document carefully before you sign it.

They talked about Stephen until they reached Canterbury.

We waited until Bruno's brother came and told us the news.

Until it happens, you tend to be complacent.

You will sleep and stay asleep until you are told to awake.

Would you mind not questioning Pauline until you have studied the journal?

Till means the same as 'until'. It is more often used in speech and informal writing.

He took a pencil out of his jacket and fumbled around till he found an old envelope.

He'll have to wait till we've finished here.

2.10 Notice that the events of time clauses introduced by 'before' and 'until' may be in doubt. Will they or did they ever happen?

At this rate we'll capsize before we get to Rocky Isle.

Before she had time to say a word, Andrew appeared.

She had put the phone down before he could press her for an answer.

People always interrupted him before he had finished what he was trying to say.

She doesn't believe anything until she has seen it in print.

He could authorize nothing until he had spoken to the new minister.

while, whilst, as, as long as

2.11 **While**, and its less frequent variant **whilst**, connect two events which happen at the same time. **As** can also have this meaning, but whereas 'while' suggests an action or state that continues for some time, 'as' often suggests a shorter action, and often means 'at that very moment'.

It was crazy that Dad was home while his wife was working.

She had just crept out while he slept.

Someone else fetches the horse whilst the owner is at work.

She grinned to herself as she lay awake in the dormitory.

As he looked at the coin, his whole expression changed.

The telephone began to ring as he unlocked the door.

'Did you get my letters?'—'I received one just as I was setting out.'

As long as sometimes expresses a similar meaning to 'while', in a more emphatic way.

I'll never forget those soldiers as long as I live.

However, it more usually has a meaning of condition. (See **2.34**.)

whenever, every time, each time

2.12 **Whenever**, **every time**, and **each time** refer to some particular circumstances that repeatedly lead to the same action happening.

I seem to catch the most appalling colds whenever I attend funerals.

Whenever this was discussed Miss Lewis became very agitated.

We go to Disneyland every time we're in Los Angeles.

Each time she went out she would buy a plant.

as soon as, immediately, the minute/second/moment...

2.13 **As soon as** and **immediately** refer to some action or event that is quickly followed by another.

As soon as he gets the money, he'll pay you.

Let me know as soon as any of them turn up.

I'll be marrying again as soon as circumstances allow.

A microphone was put under my nose immediately I got off the horse.

In more informal English, the same idea can be conveyed by expressions such as **the minute**, **the second**, and **the moment**.

I'll telephone the minute there's any change.

The moment I closed my eyes, I fell asleep.

She put down the receiver the instant she recognized my voice.

Compare **2.6**.

once

2.14 **Once**, when used as a conjunction, can also express the idea of 'as soon as' or 'when'. The main-clause event follows (and often depends on) the success or completion of the event in the subordinate clause.

The smell will disappear once the hair is dry.

Once I decided what to do, I stopped worrying.

no sooner...than, hardly...when, hardly...before

2.15 The subordinating pairs **no sooner...than**, **hardly...when**, and **hardly...before** stress how very quickly the second event follows the first. If you want to begin a clause with 'no sooner' or 'hardly', you need subject-auxiliary inversion. These expressions are used mainly in written English.

He was no sooner inside his cabin than the door opened again.

No sooner had she taken the knife from its hiding place than she dropped it.

The ambassador had hardly begun speaking when he was again interrupted by the president.

Hardly had the meeting begun when a shareholder leapt to his feet.

I'd hardly closed my eyes before I was called out again.

Time: non-finite and verbless clauses

2.16 Some time conjunctions, but not all, can introduce non-finite or verbless clauses.

'When', 'after', 'since', 'before', 'until', and 'while' can all take an '-ing'-clause.

When making records in the 1920s, sound engineers often made two recordings for safety's sake.

When lifting weights off the floor, bend your knees and keep your back straight and long.

After being colonized by Spain, Haiti was ceded to France in 1697.

It was certainly the best meal I had had since leaving home.

The people will report to you before making any major decisions.

The 65-year-old accepted his judgement until hearing a radio broadcast in 1988 about a similar case.

We decided to maximize our return on each product while hoping our superior quality would win out.

2.17 'When' and 'until' can be followed by a past participle.

Water is liquid, but when heated it becomes vapour and when frozen it is solid.

A man is guilty until proved innocent.

Grill for 15 to 20 minutes, turning occasionally until cooked.

'Once' can be followed by 'having' and then a past participle.

On the other hand, once having seen this apartment, who'd have the courage to complain?

2.18 'When', 'whenever', 'while', 'once', and occasionally 'until' can introduce verbless clauses.

The full figures, when available, will show imports remaining at a high level.

We avoided one another, whenever possible.

Greenwood continued to talk daily with Fennymore while in Florida.

Once inside her apartment she felt an urge to brush her teeth.

Cover and put in a cool place until ready to serve.

2.19 Note: in some contexts a time clause may also suggest meanings of condition, cause, or reason.

He became very lonely. He's always like that when he's away from home.

There is a gift shop selling a variety of attractive items including our own honey when available.

He was a silent man who stammered whenever he tried to talk rapidly like his friends.

She is to receive £3 million damages after a car crash left her brain-damaged.

Time: connectors

after, afterward(s), later, subsequently

2.20 These words indicate that an event takes place at a later time than a previously mentioned event or time. **After** and **afterward(s)** usually suggest a fairly short time interval between the two actions. 'After', as an adverbial connector, is used mainly in spoken English and is regarded by some people as non-standard.

It's the first time I've ever heard him talk in such a blatant fashion. After, he said 'I bet you quote that in some interview!'

Write down those ideas. We can discuss them afterwards.

We shared a cigarette. Afterward, she rested her head on my shoulder.

Later and **subsequently** imply a longer interval. 'Subsequently' is fairly formal.

At Cambridge University, he gained a first in English and later completed his PhD thesis in early 19th century poetry.

Several players needed police protection and then the remainder left the field. The referee subsequently brought them back and made them all shake hands before resuming.

before, earlier, previously, hitherto

2.21 Clauses containing these words refer to an event or situation that belongs to an earlier time than the previous sentence or clause (or than the established time context). All of them can suggest a contrast between the 'past' and 'present' time, but this idea is particularly strong with **previously** and **hitherto**. 'Hitherto' is a fairly formal word.

Now he's more focused on his work. Before, he was distracted, always making plans to go out.

She was a trifle unbalanced, perhaps even suicidal at the time. Not long before, she had attacked and beaten a complete stranger.

Several government officials were injured. Earlier, two bridges and several buildings were damaged by fires.

What about the dead man on the runway? You previously said that if any of the hostages were harmed you would move in immediately.

These expeditions marked a significant change in British policy. Hitherto they had been fighting a defensive war in Europe and America.

meanwhile, in the meantime, simultaneously

2.22 Both **meanwhile** and **in the meantime** refer to a period of time between two points, but there is a slight difference between them. 'In the meantime' emphasizes something happening or to be done while waiting until the second point is reached. If there is no particular suggestion of 'until then', but merely a reference to one activity happening 'while' another is happening, then 'meanwhile' is preferred.

'I will be back with them as soon as I can,' he promised. 'In the meantime, try to get some rest.'

The government will manage the company until it can be dismantled or sold. In the meantime, its 28 offices will remain open.

Elizabeth dried her hair and changed her clothes. Meanwhile I fiddled with the tape recorder.

Sauté the onion and celery in a small frying pan. Meanwhile melt the margarine in a saucepan.

Simultaneously, a rather formal word, indicates one action or event happening at exactly the same time as another. Unlike 'meanwhile' and 'in the meantime', it can refer to two very brief momentary events.

At that moment a vivid bolt of lightning flashed across the cove. Simultaneously a deafening crack split the air.

Of course, you can sometimes use the literal expression 'at the same time'.

The program uses so little of the computer's processing power that it is possible to do other things at the same time.

2.23 As well as the individual words and phrases discussed above, there are a large number of possible adverbial expressions which indicate when a particular event happens, linking it to a time context which has been established in an earlier sentence or clause.

He was in the Congo in 1968. After that, he made an appearance in Nicaragua in the mid 1970s.

Pioneer 10 left our solar system in June 1983. At that time it was nearly 3 billion miles from the earth.

'Why would anyone take any notice of us?' Terry said at last. At that very moment three girls cycled past.

The meaning of many of these phrases depends on a demonstrative word such as 'that'. For a full discussion of these words, see **5.4**.

Condition: conjunctions

2.24 A ***conditional clause*** explains the circumstances in which a particular thing could happen as a consequence.

Tense usage depends partly on whether we are talking about past, present, or future time, but also on how likely or unlikely the circumstances and consequences are. A modal verb is used in the main clause when we talk about an imagined situation.

if, unless

2.25 The commonest conjunction in conditional clauses is **if**. When the 'if'-clause comes first, the main clause is sometimes reinforced with 'then', particularly when it seems like a logical result. **Unless** often has the meaning of 'if. . .not'. Both 'if' and 'unless' can introduce non-finite and verbless clauses.

2.26 Sometimes the condition is a regular, typical, or normal occurrence, or was in the past. In these cases, 'if' contains a meaning of 'when' or 'whenever'.

If you tell a man of ordinary build and average strength what needs doing, he does it.

These glands all react if challenged by infection or trauma.

Unless the case is settled out of court, it can often take years before it comes to trial.

Unless otherwise stated the price of the holiday applies to each of two people sharing a room.

You had to be nice to him if you wanted to get on.

Nobody could use the computer unless they knew the password.

2.27 Sometimes a main-clause imperative is used with an 'if'-clause.

Work together, if possible.

If you want to attract schoolchildren to science and technology, make the lessons more practical.

If you are threatened with court action do not panic.

If serving the soup cold, blend the ingredients thoroughly.

2.28 Sometimes the condition may be true, or may have been true in the past, but we are not sure or don't know.

If you believe that, then you've got a very low opinion of yourself.

If you were involved in that attack, if you've been lying to me, you ought to leave straightaway.

If they are right, the universe has so little mass that its expansion is hardly slowing at all.

Unless it's in the form of insurance, the guarantee could well be worthless.

We can also speculate about events in the future.

If I accept it will be for that reason.

You don't have to let us into the property but we can get a warrant if you refuse.

The population will grow without limit unless kept in check by starvation. (...unless it is kept in check...)

A past tense is used in the conditional clause when the future event is considered unlikely. Sometimes the subjunctive 'were' is used instead of 'was'.

If I won £1 million tomorrow I'd go to my mother's house, pack her bags, and send her away.

I wouldn't have enough to live on if the operation wasn't a success.

Six out of 10 said they'd be disappointed if the President weren't deposed.

My son is the only one whom I would worry a lot about if my husband and I were to separate.

2.29 Sometimes we imagine a present or past that we know is contrary to the facts. In these cases, past tenses (or subjunctive 'were') are used in the conditional clause.

If I knew that, I shouldn't feel so helpless.

If I were in that position and thought I could win, I should certainly sue. (i.e. I am not in that position.)

If he had lived, some day Michael would have done something important. (i.e. Michael died.)

2.30 Note: 'unless' does not mean exactly the same as 'if...not'. 'Unless' stresses the condition as an exception, so more accurately it means 'except if'. You must use 'if...not' rather than 'unless' when the condition is contrary to the known facts.

It would have been comic if it had not been so frustrating. (i.e. It was frustrating.)

If the body had not been on the path it would have been ignored. (i.e. The body was on the path.)

✗ *It would have been comic unless it had been so frustrating.*

✗ *Unless the body had been on the path it would have been ignored.*

'Unless' is also not possible in sentences of the type:

I'll be glad/sorry if they do not come tomorrow.

where the truth of the main clause depends on a 'negative' action or event which is seen as a possibility, rather than an exception.

Indirect condition

2.31 'If'-clauses are sometimes used – particularly in speech – to 'soften' a statement, and the main clause statement does not in any way depend on the condition.

He looks a bit weird if you ask me.

We understand this roughly as 'If you are asking me my opinion, I think that he looks a bit weird.' But of course the speaker still thinks this even when we do not ask him or her to give an opinion!

Here are some more examples of this kind of indirect condition.

You use phrases such as 'if I may say so' or 'if you don't mind me/my saying so' when you are about to say something you think could give offence.

Utter nonsense, if I may say so.

This is an irrelevant and, if I may say so, a rather naughty remark.

You're acting a little strange, if you don't mind my saying so.

You use 'if you see what I mean' when you are trying to explain something and you feel you are not expressing yourself very well.

It isn't my fault, not really. If you see what I mean.

They seemed almost like mother and daughter, but a mother and daughter who had switched roles, if you see what I mean.

You use 'if I'm not mistaken' when you know you are right, but do not wish to appear impolite or arrogant.

And you're Mr Allan Kelling, the owner of this property, if I'm not mistaken.

If I'm not mistaken, one of the twins was named after me.

Other conditional words

2.32 There are various other less common conditional linkers, most of which only take finite verbs (**2.33–2.38**). Among these linkers are several words that are participles in form (**2.36–2.38**).

on condition that

2.33 **On condition that** stresses that something must be agreed in advance before someone will take a particular action.

He only took her to the hospital on condition that she did not say who had done this.

I reluctantly agreed to a postponement on condition that the sale should be completed and the boat handed over by 31st August.

only...if, only if, as long as, so long as

2.34 **Only...if**, **only if**, **as long as**, and its less frequent variant **so long as** can also suggest a precondition to be agreed, but more generally they suggest that particular circumstances must exist before something can happen.

A pilot will only be hired if he signs a statement to say that he will accept no orders from the passenger.

She'd only be happy if she got a thousand miles away.

My kind of magic works only if you keep on believing.

They can go into journalism for all I care as long as they're happy.

I could cook you some dinner so long as it's scrambled eggs. (i.e. Scrambled eggs is the only dish I am able or willing to cook for you.)

in the event of, in the event that

2.35 These phrases mean 'if a particular event – usually something unpleasant – happens'. This event may be considered unlikely. **In the event of** is of course a prepositional phrase, not a conjunction of any sort, and is therefore followed by a noun or an '-ing'-form. It is much commoner than **in the event that**, which is rather formal.

In the event of a foreign war or domestic agitation, what would be the resisting power of our institutions?

A life assurance scheme is one where, in return for a monthly payment over a specified period, you are guaranteed a sizeable payout in the event of your death.

Being on patrol was the only excuse I could think of in the event of my being caught at the farmhouse.

We shall give you assistance in the event that you suffer illness, personal injury or death during the period of your holiday overseas.

provided (that), providing (that)

2.36 These two conjunctions have the form of participles and are similar in meaning to 'if' or 'as long as'.

Provided that both birds are healthy I cannot see why a mating should not produce healthy chicks.

You will probably find this the most pleasant week of the diet provided you don't experience a reaction to it.

I believe in freedom to do what I wish, providing that it does no harm to my neighbour.

Mother will believe me providing I tell her what she wants to hear.

assuming (that), given that, considering (that)

2.37 **Assuming that**, or **assuming**, implies a meaning of the kind 'if we assume that one thing is true, then a second thing must also be true'.

These two basic factors must continue to apply in the future, assuming that the country remains peaceful and politically stable.

Assuming I convince you, you can convince Waddington in turn.

Given that has a similar meaning, except that there is certainty that the first thing is true.

Given that no decision is ever 100 per cent right, it's how we feel about our decisions that counts.

I don't see what I can do for you, given that you have no evidence.

Considering that, or **considering**, also introduces something that is true or certain, but the conclusion in the main clause is often rather surprising or contrasting.

Considering that they are such an important part of undergraduate courses, lectures are often presented in a remarkably poor manner.

Considering that the event had happened such a short time before, a surprising amount of information had already been collected.

These devices were very sophisticated considering they were home-made.

suppose (that), supposing (that)

2.38 As conjunctions these words imply meanings such as 'let us suppose', or 'let us imagine', so the whole sentence is concerned with considering the consequences of imaginary or hypothetical situations.

Suppose you buy a lottery ticket and then win a big prize. The moment you hear that you have won, you feel ecstatic.

Just suppose that Daniel and I were ever to get married. Would you come to the wedding?

Now supposing there were only one of those stamps, and supposing it was worth a million dollars. And supposing the man who owned it suddenly came into possession of a second stamp, its duplicate. What do you think would be the value of each of those two stamps?

Even supposing that people can agree on such choices, the result will be a rigid set of rules.

2.39 Note: as well as using subordinating conjunctions, it is possible to suggest the idea of condition in other ways:

- Conditional meaning is sometimes contained in what are apparently main clauses. Thus commands followed by 'and' can have conditional meaning.

Do that again and I'll kill you. (i.e. If you do that again, I'll kill you.)

'Or', and the more emphatic 'or else', can also conceal a threatening condition.

You will apologize or you will leave my house. (i.e. If you do not apologize, you will have to leave my house.)

Do as I say or else you'll be flying this plane alone.

- Conditional clauses are sometimes indicated not by a linking word, but by inversion of subject and auxiliary verb.

Well, I'll be in my room should you want me. (...if you want me.)

You'd be surprised were I to tell you how often that question arises. (...if I were to tell you...; ...if I told you...)

He would not have advanced the funds had he known that the balance sheet falsely indicated the firm was solvent. (...if he had known that...)

Who is the mysterious CIA major whose identity would surprise so many people did they but know it? (...if only they knew...)

(Note: the structure with 'but', shown in the above example, is rare and rather formal.)

Condition: connectors

otherwise, if not, if so

2.40 **Otherwise** and **if not** refer back to a previous statement or question, and are concerned with the consequences if it is not true or does not happen.

Your secretary told me that you would be coming over. Otherwise I should have felt compelled to call you at home. (If I had not known you were coming over, I should have felt compelled...)

You may as well go ahead with the wedding. Think of all the telephoning you'd have to do otherwise. (...if you cancelled the wedding.)

Are you pressed for time, Mr Bayliss? If not, I suggest we have lunch before going to the house.

If so also refers back, but assumes that something is true or does happen.

Does what I do scare you? If so, I will stop.

They must decide if such a plan can be implemented and if so, when.

Concession: conjunctions

2.41 Sometimes you want to combine two statements that have a rather surprising connection. To do this, you can use a ***concessive clause***; you 'concede' or admit a surprising fact that seems contrary to your main clause statement.

although, though, even though

2.42 The most common subordinating concessive conjunctions are **although**, **though**, and **even though**. These can all take non-finite or verbless clauses.

Animal tests are often used, although there is no guarantee that the results will be the same as the effects on humans.

The inquiry refused to blame the American pilots, although implying strongly they were at fault.

He produced a bottle of sherry from a cupboard and, though it was three in the afternoon, poured out glasses for all.

Though certain of ultimate victory, Haig expected the coming four months to be 'the critical period'.

I've always loved this part of London, even though it's been spoiled like everything else.

In a concessive clause with 'though', you can sometimes emphasize a particular adjective or adverb by placing it at the beginning of the clause. 'As' can be used in the same way as 'though' in this type of sentence.

Important though it is, this is not the beginning of the process.

Quietly though I had spoken, the medical superintendent heard.

Nice as this would be, reality is unfortunately different.

while, whilst, whereas

2.43 **While**, **whilst**, and the more formal **whereas** often clearly imply a contrast. 'While' and 'whilst' (but not 'whereas') are sometimes used with non-finite or verbless clauses.

She was tall with reddish hair, while I was short with dark hair.

Many Russians, whilst approving the new warmth in superpower relations, found it strange that President Gorbachev should have been mobbed as a hero.

They seem to think that brute force solves every problem, whereas you and I know it achieves little or nothing.

not that

2.44 This phrase is frequently used like a conjunction. It roughly means 'although it is not the case that...'. You can use it to add further information, often correcting a slightly wrong impression that you think someone might have. If the 'not that' clause comes first, the second clause begins with 'but'.

They won't get any fingerprints from these rubber gloves, not that any of them would know what to do with a fingerprint if they had one.

That would of course have been the end of my career. Not that it's much of a career.

'Why?'—'Well, not that you'd understand, but I can't miss this opportunity.'

'Did you smoke on the plane?' he asked slowly. 'I always do. Not that I'm nervous exactly but it helps me not to be.'

much as

2.45 **Much as** combines the meanings of 'although' and 'very much'.

Much as he longs for our marriage, he's completely absorbed in the making of maps. (Although he longs very much for our marriage...)

Compare **2.79: Manner**.

granted that

2.46 **Granted that** (another participle form) has a similar meaning to 'admittedly' or 'it is true that...'. The statement or question in the main clause is considered against the background of the subordinate clause.

Granted that killing a dog was not the sort of thing to be encouraged, it was easy to imagine that the punishment might possibly go too far.

Granted that the firm has not broken the law, is the law what it should be?

Condition plus concession: conjunctions

2.47 Some subordinating conjunctions combine a meaning of condition with concession.

even if

2.48 **Even if** is not the same as 'if'. The main-clause event or state happens in any case – and is not dependent on the condition.

Even if you know that these worries are ridiculous, at lower levels your mind remains restless and anxious. (Although you may know...)

He used to be very anxious if he had to make a speech, even if it was only a speech to his old school. (i.e. He was always anxious before making a speech; where he made the speech did not affect the situation.)

if not

2.49 This phrase introduces a reduced clause. It can combine a sense of 'even if' and 'although perhaps' something is (or was) not the case.

I lived among people who probably thought me fortunate if not rich.

She took great care to listen to the child's answers, which were emphatic if not always absolutely clear.

I breathed a little easier, if not more deeply.

The states would have the power to tax, if not the power to issue their own currencies.

whether . . . or

2.50 Here we have two contrasting conditions, but either condition 'concedes' the statement in the main clause and does not affect it in any way.

They say we're to stay on here whether we like it or not.

So these people were promoted whether or not they had any professional skills.

But who would describe herself in those terms, whether she's in her forties or seventies?

whatever, whichever, whoever, wherever, however, no matter what/who/which/how

2.51 Here we can concede any number of possible conditions; but the main-clause event always happens. Nothing makes any difference.

Whatever happened in the future, my suggestions would count for nothing.

Whatever they offer, my people will pay more.

Whichever way they fall to the ground, one sharp end has to stick up.

How she loves your new friends, darling, whoever they are!

Wherever I looked, enemies lurked.

His body began a traumatic shivering, however tightly he wrapped his arms across his chest.

No sea wall, however high and well built, is inviolable.

No matter what my friend replied, the salesman would say 'Great. Great. Glad to hear it.'

Inflation might take off again, no matter who is elected.

He always woke up early no matter how late he had gone to bed.

albeit

2.52 This is a rather rare and formal word which weakens the meaning of your main statement. It has roughly the same meaning as 'although', 'admittedly', or 'even if'. It is usually followed by some sort of abbreviated clause.

The road was packed but traffic was moving, albeit slowly.

In the United States he was a hero, albeit a somewhat tarnished one.

Concession: connectors

2.53 Connectors with meanings of concession and contrast include:

however	**though**	**even so**	**still**
nevertheless	**nonetheless**	**all the same**	

All these roughly mean 'despite this'. Note that both 'though' and 'although' are conjunctions (see **2.42**), but only 'though' can be a connector, as in the examples below. 'All the same' and 'still' are more informal than the others.

This was not an easy decision. It is, however, a decision that we feel is dictated by our duty.

There's no direct evidence that such sweeteners cause cancer. However, research into additives is going on all the time.

They even had food for a day or two. Nevertheless, he was not relaxed.

Though not generally thought of as a serious handicap in physical terms, eczema has nevertheless crippled some people's lives because of its effects.

She was hounded by a man who eventually broke into her home with a gun. Usually, though, the stalker is threatening but non-violent.

These exercises will make you more aware of how you stand, sit, lie, breathe and move. Do follow the instructions carefully, though.

You can't go on negotiating ceasefires which are quite clearly signed in bad faith. Nonetheless he will go on negotiating them.

His chances look somewhat better than his predecessor's, but even so the prolonged period of political bargaining and intrigue is not necessarily over.

Impossible, you say. All the same it has been done.

I shouldn't think you'll need me at all. But I'll be there all the same.

Without those items, the company would have come in with a $250 million loss. Still, that's a big improvement over the same quarter of one year ago.

It was a joke of course, but where exactly was the humour in saying you didn't dance very well. Still, because I couldn't see the joke didn't mean that there wasn't a joke.

anyway, anyhow, in any case, at any rate, in any event, at all events

2.54 All of these have a meaning of 'whatever happens' or 'whatever is (or was) the case'. There is therefore sometimes an element of doubt about the preceding statement. 'Anyhow' is less common than 'anyway'. 'At all events' is fairly rare.

She did fall. She said herself she tripped. Anyway, what does it matter now?

'She could at least say she isn't guilty, if she isn't.'—'I don't see why she should, since she knows very well that you're not going to believe her anyway.' (i.e. whatever she says.)

Whether it was his main subject or not I really can't remember. But anyhow he got on extremely well with the professor.

There was nothing in our agreement to keep me from showing my pictures, and the arrangement was only for a limited time, anyhow. (i.e. whatever you think was in our agreement.)

It is impossible to foretell what they may attempt. In any case, we must be prepared to meet a very strong attack.

The woman made a strange noise in her throat. It might have been speech; at any rate, the old man seemed to have understood it.

Did the General know of the plot? But in any event the General wasn't worried.

'Congratulations!', they said, 'it's an honour you deserve.'—'That's as maybe. At all events it's an honour I declined.'

See also **3.5** and **3.17**.

at least

2.55 **At least** often introduces a circumstance which stops a situation from being as bad as it possibly could be, thus implying the meaning 'so things could have been worse'.

My wallet and credit cards were stolen. At least they didn't take my passport.

Most of the crew were drowned. But at least their death was instant.

He hadn't met a single friendly face since he'd arrived. Except Katherine. She at least had a sense of humour.

See also **3.17**.

for that matter

2.56 You can use this phrase to 'concede' some extra piece of information added to an earlier statement or remark, and to emphasize that both are true.

He was only nineteen and clearly in a state of shock. For that matter, so was everyone.

I had no love for the lady. But for that matter, nobody else did either.

having said that, that said

2.57 **Having said that** and the more formal **that said** function as clauses of concession and mean roughly 'although I agree or admit what I have said'. 'Having said that' is used mainly in spoken English, but both phrases may in fact appear in writing.

Grammatically, 'having said that', like other participle clauses, should theoretically refer to the subject of the following clause, but it has become a set phrase and is often unrelated. Some people, however, consider this bad style.

Success doesn't happen overnight. Having said that, we're confident we can get the club back into the Premier League.

They do use organic ingredients whenever possible and the menu changes daily. Having said that the food is rather ordinary.

I couldn't rest my heel on the floor and work the brake at the same time. That said, taxis are very easy to drive.

Clearly, you do relate to your young man and he to you. That said, have no illusions. It might end tomorrow.

alternatively, instead, by/in contrast, conversely

2.58 These connectors of concession particularly stress the element of contrast.

Alternatively and **instead** often suggest choice.

Sieve the soup through a colander. Alternatively, liquidize it in a food processor.

There were several taxi-cabs waiting, but he decided to walk down to the main road instead.

Amy didn't look round. Instead, she was looking straight ahead of her.

By contrast and **in contrast** introduce an obvious difference.

Each territorial acquisition needed a garrison and so the army increased in size. By contrast, the size of the fleet declined.

He has virtually no experience of running anything. The other candidate, by contrast, is a sincere, caring man who made a fortune in business before going into public life.

In the larger neighbourhood I felt very unsafe. In contrast, others grow up in places where they never confronted serious danger.

Conversely is a formal word. It suggests that two events or situations are related to each other, but that opposite things happen or are true in each case.

Some people can eat more than others and still not gain weight. Conversely, some people can eat less than others and still gain weight.

Eclipses of the Moon can only occur at Full Moon: conversely, eclipses of the Sun can only occur at the time of the New Moon.

on the other hand, on the contrary

2.59 These two expressions should not be confused. **On the other hand** introduces a second argument that contrasts with what has just been said. The first argument is sometimes introduced by **on the one hand**. You can use these phrases to 'balance' an argument if you are trying to be fair and moderate.

On the one hand, I felt sorry for them, but on the other hand, I felt they knew something I didn't know.

She is not afraid of, or ashamed of, being successful, but on the other hand is prepared to sacrifice ambition for other rewards, if she so chooses.

Southern parts of Cornwall had a monthly total rainfall of less than 2 mm. On the other hand, many parts of the country suffered from thunderstorms.

On the contrary is a very strong phrase that emphasizes a contrast with the main idea of the previous statement. You can use it if you disagree with what has been said or think it is wrong.

In the end I still felt there was no way I could lose. On the contrary, I thought I would win too easily.

'You're an educated fellow. Don't you know that nothing is connected?'—'On the contrary, Mr Kennerly, everything is connected.'

Compare **then again, there again: 7.22**.

at the same time

2.60 At the same time can refer literally to two or more events happening at the same time (see **2.22**), but the phrase often introduces a slightly contradictory statement or a counter-argument to what has been said.

I was glad to be away from my difficult mother, though I missed her at the same time.

The results have been disappointing. At the same time the research is in its infancy.

despite, in spite of

2.61 Note: these are two common expressions with meanings of concession, but they are prepositions, not conjunctions or connectors. So they are followed by either a noun (or noun group) or an '-ing'-form (see **4.33**). They are never followed directly by a finite clause, but are often followed by 'the fact that' and a subordinate clause.

They wore gloves despite the fact that it was warm.

Why did you go ahead with that office party in spite of the fact that one of your employees had recently died?

Exception

except (that), only

2.62 Except that, except, and **only** introduce a clause that states an exception to the main clause.

I can't think of anything else. Except that I should have your signature as well as Roger's on these two copies.

Miss Woods said that she touched nothing in the room, except that she turned on the light.

That was when Frances started to sing: she didn't know why exactly, except it seemed the right thing to do.

I think she was as confused about him as we are, only she didn't give a damn.

otherwise

2.63 **Otherwise** sometimes means 'except for this' or 'apart from this'.

Of its recommendations, only one, that CBC operate an all-news channel, has been realized. Otherwise, little has happened.

See also **2.40**.

Purpose

to, in order to, so as to, in order for...to

2.64 Purpose is often shown by a simple infinitive clause with **to**.

A man in a gold suit and a top hat hurried forward to open the front door.

You need to put your point of view and perhaps alter your approach. To do this, you need to be firm and assertive but not aggressive.

In order to and **so as to** are more precise markers of purpose.

They need travelling papers in order to exist in the bureaucratic world.

I never drank in order to get drunk.

If we were in a decent hotel we started eating in our bedrooms so as to be alone.

She shielded her eyes so as to see him better.

You can use **in order for...to** when the subject of the infinitive clause is different from that of the main clause.

In order for her to quit there had to be some alternative occupation she could take up.

You do not have to eat hot foods in order for your body to create warmth.

so that, in order that, so

2.65 Finite clauses of purpose can begin with **so that**, **in order that**, or **so**. 'In order that' is rather formal, and 'so', without 'that', is used mainly in spoken English. Clauses of this kind often contain a modal verb.

He arranged for the taxi to come at six so that she would not have to wait long at the station.

Eat small portions so that your digestive system is not overloaded.

We only married in order that the child should be legitimate.

I went between twelve and one o'clock in order that I might find the men at home.

He may have taken up smoking early in life in order that he has something to do with his hands.

Take notes so you will remember it all.

Come to my room so I can tell you all about this wonderful play I saw in Boston.

so as not to, in order not to, so that...not, in order that...not

2.66 Clauses of negative purpose are introduced by **so as not to**, or **in order not to**. Occasionally finite clauses with **so that...not** or **in order that...not** are used.

I left quietly so as not to disturb any of the hotel guests.

He talked to the bird softly so as not to frighten it.

She slept in a separate room in order not to disturb him.

He must consume 2250 calories daily in order not to lose or gain weight.

Miss May took the little girls out of the house so that they might not hear their mother screaming.

She put down her glass in order that it should not reveal how her hand was shaking.

Reason: conjunctions

because, 'cos, since, as, for

2.67 Reason clauses are mainly introduced by **because**, **since**, **as**, and **for**. 'Because' is the commonest of these words, and is often reduced to **'cos** in informal spoken English.

Another advert has been banned from children's TV because it frightens youngsters.

Because she was my mother, I expected her to know the right choice.

What I've got in the bowl is four ounces of wholemeal self-raising flour, 'cos obviously wholemeal's better for us.

Since this is a special occasion, I've already decided to treat myself to a taxi.

The subject was mentioned, but only in passing, and since I wasn't asked to elaborate, I didn't.

'You surely know them,' I wanted to add, 'since you seem to know everyone.'

It was not a wise decision in the long run, as we had not reckoned on the dramatic rise in house prices.

'For' is formal and fairly rare in this meaning, and a 'for'-clause can only follow its main clause.

Clients are in for a shock, for they too will be subjected to new scrutiny.

in that, insofar as, to the extent that, seeing that, now that

2.68 These are some other conjunctions that introduce clauses of reason.

In that is a rather formal way of introducing an explanation.

I am an optimist in that I believe that human beings do not always perversely try to make life worse for themselves.

Most of them are not in reality engineers, in that the work they do is mostly clerical.

Insofar as (also written **in so far as**) and **to the extent that** are also formal phrases. They qualify what has been said, giving a precise reason, or perhaps the only reason, why it is true.

He didn't want power, particularly, or even money; he valued them not for themselves but only insofar as they brought him independence.

I think his offer will be received well, in so far as they will see that he wants to make some kind of a compromise.

The tenets of this sacred art exclude women to the extent that only men are allowed on the stage during a recital.

Seeing that often has a partly literal meaning: 'because someone saw or realized that' something was the case.

Seeing that I was covered with dust, she brought a bowl of hot water.

Seeing that losses on their existing loans were inevitable, the banks therefore cast around for other means of making big profits.

However, in more informal English, it sometimes has no literal meaning at all, and is used simply to introduce a reason or explanation.

Seeing that you had a police escort, the only time you could have switched cars was en route to the airport.

I'm just ringing to check everything's OK, seeing that it's Crime Prevention Week.

Now that is also partly literal, having the meaning 'because at this time'.

Now that she was retired she lived with her sister in the village of Lindleham in Berkshire.

Now that you have kept your part of the bargain, I will keep mine.

in case, lest, for fear that

2.69 **In case**, **lest**, and **for fear that** explain the main-clause action by referring to the expectations or fears of what might happen. 'Lest' and 'for fear that' are formal, and 'lest' is sometimes followed by a subjunctive.

He wasn't going to use his car in case somebody recognized it. (i.e. because somebody might recognize it, and he did not want to be recognized.)

I think I ought to stay in case Ian suddenly comes back.

I was afraid to open the door lest he should follow me. (i.e. I wanted to prevent him following me.)

British officers were forbidden to keep diaries lest they were captured and their secrets betrayed.

He refused to say anything lest he say something foolish.

They did not want to admit to any shortages of food for fear that it might reveal a weakness to be exploited by their enemies.

I said that I was ten years younger for fear that I would be turned down for the job.

Reason: connectors

2.70 If you are listing reasons you can use expressions such as **for one thing** or **in the first place**.

The Manor was a house full of interest. For one thing it was said to be haunted.

Very little was known about Lassa fever. In the first place it was difficult to recognize.

For one thing may be followed later by **for another**.

He did not immediately recognize her. For one thing, she had the sun behind her; for another, she was without her glasses.

See also **3.18–3.21: Listing**.

Result: conjunctions

2.71 A result clause must come after its main clause. Subordinate clauses indicating result are introduced by **so that**, **such that**, and **in such a way that**.

The alley was curved so that now he could not see the taxi.

Drink can suppress your appetite so that you are not eating sensibly in the first place.

She swung her shoulder bag so that it caught him full in the chest and pushed him backwards.

He actually suffered a great intolerance for alcohol, such that a single drink could produce violent, disruptive behavior.

The length and complexity of the case were such that a fair trial was not possible.

The mind reflects on itself in such a way that we become conscious of consciousness.

'So' or 'such' can be separated from 'that' and appear in the main clause. In less formal English, 'that' is often omitted.

I knew him so well that I was not surprised by this news.

Was it possible to have so much pain that it could no longer hurt?

Sometimes he was so busy thinking that he forgot to eat.

They were so surprised, they didn't try to stop him.

The champagne was of such superior quality and such a good year that she had already drunk more than she should have.

2.72 Infinitive clauses of result can be introduced by **so...as to** and **such as to.**

We are not so young or stupid as not to know our own feelings.

If a modern society is to prosper, its political, social and economic arrangements must be such as to stimulate and satisfy those with most to contribute to the common good.

Will you please act in such a way as to put their minds at rest?

Purpose or result?

2.73 Purpose and result are of course closely connected – our purpose is intended to achieve a result. 'So that' clauses of purpose are often marked by a modal verb, while result clauses usually have an 'ordinary' verb. But this is not necessarily the case, and sometimes, especially out of context, it may not be clear whether purpose or result is meant, or perhaps both are!

She also organized her eating, so that she was taking more fruit and vegetables and less starch.

2.74 For special emphasis, result can be expressed by beginning the sentence with 'so' followed by an adjective or adverb. Subject-auxiliary inversion is then required.

So successful have they been that they are moving to Bond Street.

Result: connectors

2.75 Connectors introducing a result or consequence include:

therefore	**so**	**as a consequence**
thus	**because of this**	**in consequence**
as a result	**consequently**	**accordingly**

He previously worked in the Ministry of Finance. He comes, therefore, with a great deal of experience and expertise.

These birds truly enjoy flying and should therefore be housed in lengthy aviaries.

The second millennium did not commence until January 1, 1001. Thus the second thousand years does not finish until December 31, 2000.

Most study groups are held during the day, thus avoiding evening or rush-hour travel.

Firms can contract out work to one another, and thus acquire specialized services, equipment and skills none of them could possess alone.

Only part of the restaurant was being used, and as a result the tables were closer together than usual.

On their travels they indulged their hobby of collecting antique furniture. As a result their home had become something of a museum.

Our son is at school near here, so that's another reason for not moving.

I was still unsure about the need for a book. So I consulted several academic experts on Foucault.

I travel the globe six months of every year. Because of this I honestly believe that I know more about the airline business than any of my competitors.

Both were adopted Korean girls, and because of this, felt almost like sisters.

He has attained superstar status, he has achieved a massive following and, consequently, he now has power, success and unlimited money.

The love affair itself never comes alive. Consequently, the novel's moral dilemmas fail to grip.

500,000 tourists visit the region annually. As a consequence, tourist traffic must be regulated and subjected to very tight restrictions.

Alice had to take four sleeping pills before she could get back to sleep and as a consequence failed, for the first time in her life, to turn up for a 7.00 am call.

Once Alastair got so carried away that he attempted to speak through his snorkel, and nearly drowned in consequence.

The Party identified itself with the welfare and happiness of people. It was in consequence trusted by the people.

Peace is not secured by alienating people, but rather by uniting them. Accordingly, the goal is to learn to live together in tolerance and mutual understanding.

The financing of social services affects everybody. They are, accordingly, the object of much heated discussion by economists and politicians.

hence

2.76 **Hence** may introduce a second sentence or clause, but often it introduces a word or phrase referring to something that is regarded as a result of the previous sentence or clause.

Linguistics, then, is the field which classifies the pronunciation, grammar, meaning and use of language and hence provides terminology to talk about these matters.

My guess is somebody on our side arranged it, some dirty tricks operation; hence the deathly silence.

thereby

2.77 **Thereby** also means 'as a result' or 'in this way', but it is not used at the beginning of a new sentence.

She hit the soldier's outstretched arm, and thereby saved the life of a demonstrator whom he was about to shoot at point-blank range.

Smokers stay longer in hospital, thereby depriving non-smoking patients of treatment.

then, in that case, in which case

2.78 **Then** introduces a logical deduction or obvious conclusion.

'I have not stolen any money.'— 'Then you must know who did.'

If this argument is right, then there are many new things to worry about.

In that case introduces a result that follows naturally or automatically if we assume that the previous statement is true. If the previous statement suggests real uncertainty or hypothesis, you say **in which case**.

'I'm sure all the obvious methods have been checked.'—'In that case there's not much I can do.'

Either I know my job, in which case I shall know the answer to your questions. Or else I don't know my job, in which case I probably shouldn't be here.

Manner: conjunctions

2.79 Clauses of manner explain how something is done, that is, the way it is done.

As and **like** roughly mean 'in the same way as' or 'in a similar way to'. They may be preceded by 'just', in the sense of 'exactly'. 'Like', with this function, is used mainly in spoken English, and is considered incorrect by some people.

In the end I could always do as Harry had suggested. I could go to the press and tell the story.

The round clock at the rear of the room ticked loudly, just as I remembered.

I mean, like you said last night, the fact that you're a soldier doesn't mean to say that you want to kill.

Much as means 'in roughly the same way as'.

She grasped the pen in her fist with the point down, much as a young child would do.

I serve my country much as you serve yours.

The jury will decide pretty much as you tell them to, won't they?

as if, as though, like

2.80 **As if** and **as though** suggest a sort of comparison, which may be imaginary, or may alternatively indicate someone's impression or belief about something. Both can introduce non-finite clauses. **Like**, when used with this meaning, is very informal and is often considered to be incorrect.

You talk as if she was someone you once knew.

She said the word as if the meaning escaped her.

They looked at me as though I hadn't a clue to the meaning of activism.

She lifts his hand as if to lead him somewhere.

He paused and looked round the room as if saying goodbye to it.

Lucas stepped toward the burnt house as though hypnotized.

You sound like you remember them.

2.81 Manner clauses are also introduced by phrases such as **the way**, **in a way**, or **in the way**. 'Way' is sometimes followed by 'that'.

People like you the way that you are.

You end up making a happier life for yourself by understanding yourself in a way you never have before.

He treated Haig's suggestions as if they were commands, probably in the way they were intended.

Then you can paint your nails in the way you apply nail varnish.

These cats and dogs caught birds in the way they might, in Europe, have caught mice.

Place: conjunctions

2.82 If you need to use a clause rather than a simple adverb to refer to the place or position in which something happens, you can use a clause beginning with **where**, **wherever**, or **everywhere**.

I'm so glad to see you back where you belong.

Where the lane ends, continue on a narrow woodland footpath which rises briefly before running downhill.

Ramesh can take this document wherever he likes to have it checked.

Collect Mrs Selby and take her wherever she wants to go.

Everywhere I went in Tibet, Tibetans kept remarking on the strange weather.

2.83 In many verbless clauses beginning with 'where' or 'wherever', the meaning is not so much of place, but of time and condition.

Even after the military takeover a week ago, the people wherever possible continued to encourage us. (i.e. when and if it was possible.)

The local committees draw up lists of qualified practitioners who can test sight and make up glasses where necessary.

Comparison: conjunctions

2.84 ***Comparative clauses*** compare one thing or person with another. They are of two kinds:

- Clauses based around the idea that the things or people are equal (or not equal) in terms of some quality that they possess.
- Clauses that emphasize difference, stating that one thing or person has more or less of a particular quality than the other.

In comparative clauses, there is usually either ellipsis (i.e. omission) of elements in the main clause, or substitution (e.g. using a phrase with the verb 'do' instead of repeating the verb phrase).

as...as, not as...as, not so...as

2.85 Comparisons of equality use **as...as**.

She was just as rude to the boys as the girls. (...as she was to the girls.)

One fetched for oneself and ate as much as one could (...as one could eat.)

John Kempton was now as strong as could be expected. (...as it could be expected that he would be.)

He's as angry as anybody at the news.

Either **not as...as** or **not so...as** is used to indicate inequality.

She wouldn't have known her as well as you did.

The job was not as difficult as the look of the place implied.

She was not so innocent as he'd first thought.

-er...than, more...than, less...than

2.86 Clauses emphasizing difference are introduced by **than** preceded by a comparative form.

Well there can be some girls that are better than boys but mostly the boys are cleverer than girls.

It is easier to arouse a tiger than to ride it.

He was back sooner than she expected.

The comparative expression often includes the words **more** or **less**.

He felt more tired than he had ever felt.

I've already said more than I intended to say.

I've been wrong much more often than I've been right.

Tony looked more tanned and handsome than ever. (...than he had ever looked.)

The new men, not wanting to appear less tough than the veterans, kept silent.

The prospect is ultimately less attractive than it seems.

2.87 When only the subject of a second clause remains after 'as' or 'than', and it is a pronoun, some people insist that a subject pronoun must be used.

She is just as foolish, as stupid, as impulsive as I. (...as I am.)

However, this is formal. 'As' and 'than' can be considered in this sort of context as prepositions, and object pronouns, with subject meaning, are common and not wrong.

They're fighting the same war as us. (...as we are.)

She arrived earlier than him. (...than he did.)

Proportion

2.88 There are two rather unusual types of two-clause sentences which express a kind of comparison, but also include an idea of result:

- The first type consists of parallel clauses, each beginning with **the** followed by a comparative form.

The more I thought about it, the more confused I became.

He is the most versatile actor on TV. The more shows he does the better. (i.e. He should do more shows.)

The more stress one experiences, the higher the cholesterol levels tend to be.

He believed that the less you said, the more likely you were to be heard.

- The other type of sentence is fairly rare. The first clause begins with **as** and the second with **so**. What is happening in the second clause depends in some way on what is happening in the first clause, and takes place at the same time.

As the genetic secrets of muscle growth unfold, so the prospects for genetically manipulating muscle fibres improve.

As the cost of keeping money in the bank increases, so it's spent faster.

Preference

2.89 You can express preference using another unusual type of clause, beginning with **rather than**, or occasionally **sooner than**. These clauses are followed by a bare infinitive (not a finite verb).

Rather than engage in a long report over the telephone, I had invited him to lunch with me at home on this quiet Sunday.

Rosemary had thought it important enough to come herself, rather than send one of the maids.

They will sink us sooner than permit our safe arrival in any British port.

3 Connectors: explaining

3.1 There are some connectors which have meanings that are not related to the meanings expressed in adverb clauses introduced by a conjunction. Sometimes you use these connectors to signal that you are going to explain further what you have said – by adding more information, giving examples, rewording, listing, or summing up.

Adding

3.2 Co-ordinating conjunctions such as 'and', and co-ordinating pairs such as 'not only . . . but also' can of course have an 'adding' meaning. So in a sense do all connectors, since they all add some information. But some connectors particularly signal that they are adding information or a further argument **(3.3–3.12)**.

moreover, furthermore, further

3.3 These three words are all fairly formal, though fairly common, ways of signalling that you are adding information, or some extra support for the point you are making.

Most streets in Tokyo are safe at night. Moreover, the juvenile crime rate actually has fallen in recent years.

They seem to know exactly what they're doing and, moreover, make you want to admire them for it.

The organization has both limited powers and limited funds. Furthermore, it has no right of access to countries outside the treaty.

His enormous reputation is almost entirely posthumous. It is based, furthermore, on very little actual production.

No single British field sport has been subjected to abolition by law. Further, hunting with hounds continues to thrive throughout the British Isles.

in addition, additionally, what is more, on top of that

3.4 These are some other connectors which you can use to add information. **In addition** is the most frequent.

He is incapable of using rhythm and pace for dramatic effect. In addition, he stumbles over words.

Even on the simplest voyage there is a feeling of adventure and excitement. When, in addition, you are in your own boat you realize just how lucky you are.

Banks are run by people, and people make mistakes. Additionally, like all industries, banks will have their share of dishonest workers.

Barely three months later they are engaged in an unholy row. What is more, it is a row over basic principles.

On top of that is rather informal.

That day the heat was unbearable, and on top of that, tsetse flies bit me every time I slowed down.

I won't tell a lie on your behalf. And on top of that, it's the stupidest lie I've ever heard.

You'll be interviewed, of course. On top of that, we'd like you to describe what happened in your own words.

besides, anyway, anyhow

3.5 Besides adds information, sometimes emphasizing an additional or important point, sometimes offering an explanation of what has been said.

The doctors couldn't talk English and besides they were never around.

I want to share my paintings with my clients. Besides, my apartment is too small for them all.

Martin sat on the bank at one side of the lay-by, watching the parked lorries and waiting. Besides he was tired.

Anyway and **anyhow** can also share this meaning.

It's not joyriding, anyway. It's stealing, isn't it?

We cut all scenes of sex and violence because it is against our religion. Anyway, it's bad for the children.

I though it was best to warn him. Anyhow, Cheryl wanted him to know.

after all

3.6 After all introduces a further explanation or justification for the previous statement, which itself has tried to explain something that might seem slightly unusual or puzzling.

Her speaking in German was hardly peculiar. After all, it was her native tongue.

Her contradictions were not so unusual, not if you stopped to think about it. Most people, after all, were a mix of good and evil.

I'm not advising you to throw away your makeup or forget about your appearance. After all, we do live in a world where beauty counts.

Do not confuse this very special meaning with 'finally' or 'lastly' **(3.23)**.

above all

3.7 Above all adds a point that is more important than anything that has been said.

And it's far from silent there. Above all, of course, there's the singing of the the birds and the squeaks and rustling movements of small animals.

Rather than a 70 mph limit she said a better idea might be a device that automatically restricted cars to the speed limit. Above all, the association wants a change in car advertising.

indeed

3.8 Indeed adds a further comment that emphasizes the truth of what has already been said.

The Great Bear rotates about the sky and is always visible at night in the Northern Hemisphere. Indeed, during a total eclipse, it is visible in the daytime as well.

Those with chapped hands should try treating them with my special herb lotion. Indeed, the lotion is so safe that it can even be recommended for treating swollen eyes.

to cap it all, to top it all

3.9 To cap it all and **to top it all** are occasionally used to introduce some final and rather surprising item.

We had frosts in April and May. To cap it all we even had nights of frost in June.

They have little or nothing of value left to sell. And to top it all, some have also been beaten up by the airport security guards.

also, too, as well

3.10 Also occasionally begins a sentence when another reason is being given.

I can't remember ever being bored. Also, Anastasia, I can't remember you ever complaining of boredom before.

Please be as generous as you can with extra donations. It is also helpful if you subscribe by Banker's Order.

You cannot begin a sentence with **too** or **as well**; indeed, they often come at the end.

Oh I do feel ill. My arm hurts, too.

He was just another child from the shelters. There were other children as well.

Write down what is said or done and when. Ask a friend or colleague to take a note as well.

similarly, likewise

3.11 If you want to add some fact or detail that parallels what you have said, you can use **similarly** or **likewise**. They roughly mean 'in the same way'.

The only reason he used a rental car company more than once was that there weren't enough to avoid repetition. Similarly, he never used the same passport twice, nor the same credit cards.

The job has given me great pleasure and has taken me to places I would not otherwise have visited. Likewise I have made marvellous friends and acquaintances.

Working women, especially if they have children, may not have time for community activities. Likewise working men.

equally

3.12 If you want to add that some other, parallel situation is true or relevant to the same degree, you can use **equally**.

In that situation, he would lie. Equally in my situation I would want to believe he was lying.

What will the 19,000 Syrian troops do? And equally, what will the 10,000 French troops do?

Giving examples

3.13 If you want to indicate that you are going to give an example of something you are talking about you can use **for example**, **for instance**, or **e.g.** The abbreviation 'e.g.' stands for the Latin expression 'exempli gratia' (meaning 'for example'). Originally it was a written convention, but is nowadays commonly used in spoken English.

Most of us can take simple precautions to minimise the risk. For example, we avoid walking in parks or deserted city areas after dark.

He seemed unaware of some rather basic details about you. For example, what you look like.

The new test has some similarities to a conventional IQ test, but also some significant differences, It does not, for instance, have a test of vocabulary.

Recognizing priorities is another vital ingredient to the effective use of time. For instance, at home you may be faced with several jobs which need attention, e.g. cooking the evening meal, ironing clothes for tomorrow, housework, washing the car.

Rewording

3.14 Sometimes you try to make your meaning clearer by repeating what you have said in a different way. There are several connector phrases which enable you to do this. Of course, when you use such a phrase you may simply be rewording your original remark, but you may, in fact, be adding more information or you may be correcting what you have said, or even just saying something rather different!

in other words, that is to say, that is, i.e., namely

3.15 These are the main connectors that you can use to indicate that you are rewording what you have just said or written. The abbreviation **i.e.** stands for the Latin 'id est' (meaning 'that is'), and, like 'e.g.', it has spread from the written language to ordinary spoken English. **Namely** is more often found in writing than in speech.

For the past century or so, geologists have worked on the basis that the present is the key to the past. In other words, they use processes familiar today to explain how ancient rocks formed.

The onus is on the shopkeeper to provide goods which live up to the quality of their description; in other words, they must not be bad or off.

A film is made at twenty-four frames a second. That is to say that the camera takes twenty-four photographs each second.

A portrait painter or a landscape artist fakes, that is to say he rearranges nature to a better angle for his purpose.

Then I didn't hear a thing from them until yesterday, that is, the last day of February.

Some teachers may be more effective than others because they explain better. That is, they employ qualitatively different kinds of verbal interaction with students.

And please don't say anything until we're there; that is, if we ever get there.

Anyone could learn this way. Any man, that is.

The advertisement was taken as it was intended, i.e. straight-talking and fair.

Many ponies are kept at grass livery, i.e. they live outside all year round.

He held the receiver to his ear long enough to establish what he already knew, namely that the line was cut.

...the shortage of housing in the area to which he decided to move, namely Tower Hamlets.

Correcting

or rather, or better still

3.16 If you want to reword more carefully something you have said, and you want to point out that you are in fact correcting your remark, you can use **or rather**, **or better still**, or a similar phrase.

I explained to him how far things had got, or rather had not got.

They were astonished at men marching up with such courage, or rather madness, to certain death.

Beneath the conscious mind are all the manifold levels of what is called the unconscious, or better, the subconscious mind.

You should think of your customers as partners, or better still, family.

Maria was standing in the doorway of the apartment, or more correctly, leaning against one side of it.

at least, anyway

3.17 At least and **anyway** are sometimes used to qualify a statement. Therefore they can sometimes suggest a correcting meaning.

Mums and Dads do help their children. As far as I can see. I help mine or at least I think I used to.

I couldn't promise to marry him. Not yet, anyway.

Listing

3.18 If you want to emphasize the points you are making, you can use a ***listing connector***. The main listing connectors are discussed in paragraphs **3.19–3.24**.

first, second, third...
firstly, secondly, thirdly...

3.19 These apparently time-related words (with the exception of 'first' – see **3.20**) are used almost exclusively to list points or reasons.

There were always two certainties about 1993. First, that devaluation and interest rate cuts would bring an economic upturn. Second, that it would bring the Government some political relief.

He was disappointed in the lack of action after his speech. 'First, I wanted the government to acknowledge what I had said, and they didn't. Secondly, I expected the local authority to try to do something about it.'

They are angry with me firstly because I went to the United States, secondly because I didn't come back after the war and thirdly because I came back.

...Secondly, a lot of junk mail emanates from abroad. Thirdly, we would be unable to impose realistic sanctions on transgressors. Fourthly, I feared that the deluge of extra work would swamp our decidedly finite resources. (i.e. The writer is explaining why it would be impractical to make junk mail illegal.)

first, then, next

3.20 First, **then**, and **next** – and occasionally other words (e.g. 'second') – can be used to indicate the order in which events occur in time, so they are sometimes used when listing a series of instructions. 'First' links the earliest of the actions to the others. 'Then' and 'next', like 'after' and 'afterwards' (see **2.20**), may suggest only a short interval between events, or virtually no interval.

First, the organization sought and found young people with talent. Then they assessed them for other capacities.

First he loosened the pin on the grenade. Next he wired the body of the grenade to the door handle.

First, the buyer/seller approaches a stockbroker or commercial bank and instructs them to buy or sell a specific number of shares in a particular company. Second, the stockbroker or bank approaches a market maker to buy or sell the shares as instructed.

Let your arms slowly drift down to your sides again. Then, slowly screw them up into fists. Hold tight like that, and then relax again. Next, your back.

Gallagher secured the paddles inside the canoe. Next he hung Onyschuk's backpack from the branch of a tree.

first of all, in the first place

3.21 **First of all** is an emphatic phrase, and means 'before anything else'. It can refer to either time or reason.

First of all, I'm going to explain what I believe is going on.

It was a marvellous place to begin one's management career. First of all, there were so many different aspects of transport on which to try my hand.

However, **in the first place** almost always introduces a reason.

No, sir, that wouldn't work, and you know it. In the first place your interests and Miss Radcliffe's may not totally coincide. Second, in the course of my investigation I may uncover information detrimental to her reputation.

In the first place she didn't want to leave him. Secondly, she had no intention of abandoning any part in the film he was producing.

A tight authoritarian system isn't going to work in the first place and, in the second place, if they try to adopt it, there's nobody to support them.

to start with, to begin with, for a start

3.22 Like most of the phrases discussed in the previous paragraphs, these phrases too can refer to time or reason.

Aim at a short walk to start with, say for 20 minutes on flat ground. Then begin to increase your speed and distance. Eventually you should be able to take a brisk walk at least three times a week.

To begin with I thought of Terry as a really nice, fun person. Then one day he said he was seriously in love with me.

'What should I write down?'—'The precise name of the wine, for a start.'

You've been listening to too much propaganda, young man. So now you're going to hear the truth. To start with, our civilization is older than yours.

This really was a romance, but the obstacles were insurmountable. To begin with, they were both married.

After the engine was in full production it was discovered that it was a major disaster. For a start, it weighed not 600 but 656 pounds.

finally, lastly, last but not least

3.23 When you are listing – whether you are recounting activities in order of time, or reasons, or anything else – you can signal that you are reaching the end of your list by using **finally** or **lastly**. (Notice 'then', used purely as a listing word, in the first example.)

Then there are the needs of the individuals. We all like to be praised and to fulfil our ambitions. Finally, there are the needs of the team which must work as a cohesive unit.

Working for too long a time, without adequate rests or change, is likely to cause errors to increase and lead you to become otherwise inefficient, generating yet more work. Lastly, overwork can be a way of masking other problems.

Cream the butter and sugar to a smooth consistency and gradually add the egg whites. Lastly blend in the flour and vanilla essence.

Last but not least means that though you are mentioning something last, it is in fact important, not some afterthought.

We thank the Mental Health Foundation, British Heart Foundation, and the Chest, Heart and Stroke Association for supporting our research. Last but not least, we thank the patients themselves without whose enthusiasm and personal experience this book would not have been written.

Problems can come from photocopier fluids, solvents, aerosols, cleaning agents, air purifiers and, last but not least, the fabric of the building and its furnishings.

one final point, a final point

3.24 To signal the end of an argument or list of reasons, you can also use **one final point** or **a final point**, though these phrases are not, of course, connectors.

> *Thirdly, I always find that live interviews with interesting people add zest and sparkle to any piece of research. One final point is that I actually knew a good deal about some of these subjects myself before writing this book.*

> *A final point I'd like to make about the grip is the position of my right index finger.*

Summing up

to conclude

3.25 You can use **to conclude** before making a final point, but as people often like to summarize something they have said, you can also use this phrase before summing up. This is a fairly formal expression, appropriate in a book or a lecture.

> *To conclude, I would like to make some points about Christian mysticism as a whole.*

> *To conclude, seapower was once more a vital component of the British and American conduct of the war.*

all in all, to sum up, in conclusion, altogether

3.26 If you want to summarize what you have been saying, or point to the conclusion that you consider your arguments or statements prove, these are some of the various words and phrases you can use.

> *Ten years now she'd been alone, but she'd spent them usefully. She enjoyed her life and had some good friends in the village. All in all, she'd been very lucky.*

> *...In difficult and chronic cases changes were brought about only through this type of treatment. To sum up, many people were helped through this treatment and most of them were people with chronic conditions.*

> *...Pedometers are not too expensive and are available from most sports shops. In conclusion, walking is a cheap, safe, enjoyable and readily available form of exercise.*

> *I like Peter very much. He's amusing, clever, and enlightened. Altogether a charming fellow.*

in short

3.27 You can use **in short** if you are going to sum up something in a very few words.

I want to believe you are wholly innocent of those boys' deaths. I want to believe you never played about with drugs or silly games. In short, I want to believe you are a victim.

By the time of President Tito's death, in short, federal institutions were fatally weak.

We had a record player and a few records, and we used to make a lot of noise going out into the hall to fetch water for tea. In short, girls having fun.

Stating your topic

as for

3.28 Sometimes you may want to change the subject slightly, by referring to a different but related topic. One way of doing this is to use the prepositional phrase **as for** followed by a noun group or an '-ing'-form.

His other major victories came in 1988 and 1989. As for the future, Fignon would say little.

Dr Maturin could speak fluently in Latin and Greek, and as for modern languages, to Jack's certain knowledge he spoke half a dozen.

She was finished with 'good works'. As for going back to the United States, that was impossible.

as regards, as to

3.29 **As regards** and **as to** are similar phrases for changing the subject slightly, or talking about another aspect of the same topic.

There was a lab at the college and I did a little experimental work in botany there. As regards research, there were just no grants at all.

This makes it difficult to ascertain the exact time of death. However, it is thought that a more detailed post mortem will give the answer. As to motive, police are still baffled.

with reference to

3.30 **With reference to** is a formal way of stating your topic. It is sometimes used at the beginning of formal letters, here a letter to a scientific journal. But although the phrase may occur at the beginning of a text (unlike 'as for' and 'as to') it is of course referring back to some earlier letter or article with which the reader of the letter is expected to be familiar.

> *With reference to J.C.A.Craik's third rainbow, I have been intrigued by a related phenomenon, that of seeing a rainbow apparently reflected in a water surface.*

4 Relative clauses, 'that'-clauses, 'wh'-clauses, and others

4.1 As mentioned in **1.22**, subordinate clauses include not only adverb clauses but also relative clauses, 'that'-clauses, and 'wh'-clauses. 'That'-clauses and 'wh'-clauses are sometimes referred to collectively as noun clauses. There are also various non-finite and verbless structures that function in a similar way to finite subordinate clauses.

Relative clauses

4.2 You often give further information about someone or something by using an adjective. But sometimes this is not enough, and you can then use a ***relative*** (or 'adjectival') ***clause***. The relative clause comes immediately after the noun (or pronoun) it qualifies.

Relative clauses usually begin with one of the relative pronouns 'who', 'whom', 'whose', 'which', or 'that'.

There are two main types of relative clause, ***defining*** and ***non-defining***.

Defining relative clauses

4.3 A ***defining relative clause*** gives essential information that 'defines' or identifies the person or thing you are talking about.

When the pronoun is the subject of the relative clause, you use 'who' or 'that' for people:

> *I'm looking for someone who might be able to help me.*
>
> *Women who have this condition are often overweight.*
>
> *Do we want the people that use the beaches to pay for it?*

and 'which' or 'that' for things:

> *The office which had been cleared for them was austere but functional.*
>
> *It can be seen now as an unnecessary and grave mistake which led to a political disaster.*
>
> *Jealousy is an energy that takes us over.*
>
> *Think of a word that sums up how you feel.*

4.4 When the relative pronoun is the object in its clause, you use 'whom', 'who', or 'that' for people. Strictly speaking 'who' is incorrect as an object pronoun, but it is increasingly used, and 'whom' is felt to be formal.

> *And then there was Clara, that woman whom Clarence had married.*
>
> *Also with them was a woman friend who I last saw thirty years ago.*
>
> *Many of the youngsters who we have helped are now married.*
>
> *After all that killing, it's enough to be alive and well with someone that you love and trust.*

When the object is a thing, you use 'which' or 'that'.

> *Grace sat down in the leather chair which her brother had originally offered her.*
>
> *The kind of music that David Bowie and Brian Eno were doing was very much in the direction of experimental music.*

As a further option, you can often omit the object pronoun completely.

> *It is a portrait of a person_we don't know.*
>
> *That bestseller book_I wrote made me a lot of money.*
>
> *He never listened to a thing_I said.*

4.5 When a relative pronoun functions as the object of a preposition, you can use 'that' (for both people and things) if the preposition comes at the end of the clause.

> *A lot of people must have looked carefully at the person that they were living with.*
>
> *We're very much interested in the background of the people that we're talking to.*
>
> *Take the statistics of science that we looked at earlier.*

Alternatively, the pronoun can be omitted altogether.

> *No matter how hard they work, the person_they are responsible for is working twice as hard.*
>
> *There was no one else_he could talk to.*
>
> *The only thing_I'm concerned about is reusable products.*

But if the preposition precedes the pronoun, you must use 'whom' for people and 'which' for things.

> *The only people with whom he could discuss the plan were those who knew of it already.*

She would be safe in Jehol now, with her dying Emperor and the little son through whom she hoped to rule China.

The book stands as a monumental testimony to the historical circumstances in which it was written.

This is something for which you must constantly be on the lookout.

Non-defining relative clauses

4.6 A ***non-defining relative clause*** adds extra information about someone or something, but who or what they are is already clear. Non-defining relative clauses are more common in writing than in speech, and they are separated from the rest of the sentence by a comma or commas.

4.7 You use 'who' (subject) or 'whom' (object) for people, and 'which' for things. Non-defining relative clauses are a more formal structure than defining ones, so 'whom' is preferred to 'who' in object position.

My brother, who is a gourmet, took him on tours of France.

Unfortunately Frank Wolf, who would never have agreed, was away at the time.

He spent much of the evening with Walter Cronkite, whom he had hardly seen in the thirty years since they had worked together at CBS.

Paul's father, with whom he had had a close relationship, died suddenly.

Flex your knees so that your feet, which should be together, are flat on the floor.

Well I remember, for example, our meetings in London in 1954, which you certainly remember.

Today the menu consisted of smoked salmon mousse, with which they were drinking a delightful white wine.

whose

4.8 **Whose** means 'of whom' or 'of which', and describes ownership or some other close relationship. You can use it in defining and non-defining clauses, and it can refer to people and to things.

He was an officer whose career meant everything to him.

He married a woman whose name I forget.

There is a wonderful story about Lord Uxbridge, whose leg was shot off at the Battle of Waterloo.

Even a state like Austria-Hungary, whose very existence depended on balance and law, was affected by the dominance of military strategic thinking.

For repairing a modern, hardback book whose cover has fallen off, they charge about £15.

The butcher shot pigeons and sold them to the people on whose land he had shot them.

4.9 In written English you can construct a relative clause using a pronoun such as 'some', 'each', or 'many', followed by 'of whom', 'of which', or 'of whose'.

The room was packed with people, many of whom Amy had never seen before.

He devotes most of his words to two topics: money and health, each of which he seemed to lack in equal measure.

He remains a great admirer of Warhol, several of whose pictures he now owns.

Numbers, as well as comparative and superlative phrases, can be used in the same way.

They heard voices ahead, two voices, one of which suddenly rose above the other in anger.

There are 50 families here. Between them they only have 11 family names, five of which go back to the names of the original settlers.

They have two sizes of mixing bowl, the larger of which inverts over the scales for easy storage.

She gave birth to eight children, the youngest of whom died in 1954.

Alternatively, 'of' can come at the beginning of the relative clause, changing the word order slightly.

Her haunting landscapes, of which many were painted in the Dordogne, seem to express a profound sense of fear and foreboding.

He had fifteen children of whom three went into the Army.

For reduced relative clauses, see **4.27**.

when, where, why

4.10 **When** and **where** sometimes function as relative adverbs, in both defining and non-defining clauses. See also **2.6**.

Magnus is there waiting for the day when we shall be together.

He showed me maps of his country and the place where his family had a country house.

We live in the mountains, where life is hard.

Similarly, **why** is sometimes used after the word 'reason'. 'That' (or nothing at all) may also be possible.

There must be some reason why he looked pleased.

The reason that they liked the restaurant was its anonymity.

That is the reason _ I asked you.

whereby

4.11 **Whereby** is a formal conjunction, roughly meaning 'by which' or 'in which way'. You can use it when you want to explain how something such as a system, process, or plan happens.

A routine was established whereby the men worked in the mornings and played football in the afternoons.

Poirot and Hastings had devised a plan whereby one or the other would leave the hotel first; then, after an interval, the other would follow.

This is the system whereby the European Union automatically gets the cash from some British taxes.

Other relative clauses

4.12 You can use a relative clause to say something happened after something else.

There was laughter again, which the corporal silenced.

The left hand still held a pair of pliers, which Kelly took and used to tighten the wire yet more.

The new aircraft design was submitted to the Ministry, who promptly rejected it on the grounds that there was no immediate requirement for it.

4.13 You can use a clause beginning with 'which' to comment on the whole of the preceding clause.

He was probably talking to himself, which he often did now.

Her only commitment tomorrow is a rehearsal at the Conservatoire during the afternoon. Which means the morning is the time to make contact.

She looked like a ghost, by which I mean that she seemed not entirely alive.

Noun clauses

4.14 'Wh'-words and 'that' are not only used to introduce relative clauses. You can also use them to introduce a type of clause that functions rather like a noun or noun group, for example as the subject, object, or complement of a verb. In such cases, both types of clause are often referred to as ***noun clauses*** (or ***nominal clauses***). The following examples illustrate how such clauses are related to noun groups:

We didn't like the hotel. (ordinary noun group)

We didn't like the hotel we stayed in. (noun group with relative clause)

We didn't like where we stayed. ('wh'-clause as noun clause)

In the paragraphs below, where the same point applies to 'that'-clauses and 'wh'-clauses, we shall, where appropriate, use the term ***noun clause*** to cover both types of clause, for the sake of convenience.

The term 'wh'-clause also includes clauses beginning with 'how'.

4.15 One very common use of noun clauses is as objects in report structures, after verbs of reporting and thinking.

He explained that he couldn't be more specific.

She said that she'd had a card from him.

He explained how the climate was just right for growing sugar.

In structures of this kind, 'that' is often omitted from a 'that'-clause.

She said_she knew nothing of thc plans.

When he took the job people agreed_he was a good choice.

Reported questions use a 'wh'-clause or an 'if'-clause.

Finally she asked what I'd brought with me.

I wonder who he's with.

A stewardess enquired whether he really was Mr H. Hughes.

I asked if we could stay for a while.

(For full details see *Collins COBUILD English Guides 5: Reporting*.)

4.16 The name ***nominal relative clause*** is sometimes given to a special type of 'wh'-clause that does not represent a question, and which, unlike other nominal clauses (that have an abstract meaning), can refer to either people or things. A nominal relative clause functions like a noun or noun group, but it is also partly like a relative clause; the 'wh'-word has a double function and means 'that which', 'the thing(s) which', or 'the person(s) who'.

What you need is a change of scene.

The driver will take you to your address to let you get your passport and to pack what you need.

That's who I'm paying the rent to.

Whatever I did there was motivated by fear.

Whoever did this must be caught.

You know where I'll be. (...the place where...)

However, the distinction between 'pure' noun (or nominal) clauses and nominal relative clauses is not always clear, and both have the same sort of function in a sentence. The terms noun clause and 'wh'-clause in paragraphs **4.17–4.23** therefore cover both types.

4.17 As well as functioning as the object in a report structure, a noun clause can function as the object of other (non-reporting) verbs. 'That' is sometimes omitted. 'Wh'-clauses can be non-finite.

He saw that a police car was parked outside.

He doesn't mind who uses it.

Anxiously, Gill looked up at the clouds to see which way the wind was blowing.

I suggest you call whichever girlfriend you had your eye on for the weekend and warn her you'll be working.

That shows how desperate she is.

Over the years I've learnt to remember how to survive, and how to forget pain.

4.18 Noun clauses can also function as complements, for example after the verb 'be'.

The fact is that I'm going to get married.

The fact is we couldn't think of anything else to do.

My problem, put baldly, is that I've doubts about Carmela's suicide.

I hope that wasn't why he was so angry.

Yes, Andy Holden was who I meant.

4.19 A noun clause can also function as the subject of a sentence. In such cases the sentence often begins with a dummy, impersonal 'it', and the noun clause follows. 'That' can be omitted from a 'that'-clause when there is a dummy 'it'.

It emerged that they shared a mutual passion for sailing.

It was odd he had no means of identification at all.

It was a mystery to me why he never appeared to be especially popular with his colleagues.

Alternatively, the noun clause can come at the beginning of the sentence (with no dummy 'it'). This pattern is fairly common with 'wh'-clauses, but relatively rare in the case of 'that'-clauses. The 'that' must not be omitted from a 'that'-clause which begins a sentence.

What he did at home was perhaps even more remarkable.

That he was rescued at all was a matter of coincidences.

4.20 'Wh'-clauses sometimes follow a preposition.

She crossed to where he stood.

Their father often reminisced about when he had worked as a New York City police detective.

Afterwards you can talk to whoever you like.

It was no longer a case of who would win, but when. (...but of when.)

There was no record of whom she had phoned.

4.21 'That'-clauses and 'wh'-clauses can follow some adjectives.

Fowler was angry that the contract had not been placed with his firm.

I really am glad I decided to come.

I can't even be sure how old those bones are.

4.22 Noun clauses, especially 'that'-clauses, can also be used ***in apposition to*** a noun group, as an explanation of that noun. This often happens with nouns related to reporting and thinking (e.g. 'fact', 'belief') and with some other nouns (e.g. 'danger', 'possibility').

The fact that many of us eat too much junk food can hardly have escaped anyone's notice.

He had condoned it at first in the belief that he was genuinely helping further the cause of science.

The producer may then use the logo on the wine label as evidence that the wine is 'verified' as organic.

There was a danger that many of the country's important foreign workers would decide to leave.

They called their child Indiana, prompting the question, what's wrong with a good old English name?

4.23 Note: 'that'-clauses sometimes look like relative clauses, but their function is different.

He had heard rumours that old Fritz's heart wasn't as good as it used to be. ('that'-clause in apposition)

I am aware of the rumours that have recently been circulating about me. ('that' introducing relative clause)

Non-finite and verbless clauses

With conjunctions

4.24 Adverbial conjunctions that can take non-finite and verbless clauses are described in Chapter 2. Such clauses can often be seen as a sort of reduced clause with the subject and part of the verb 'be' omitted.

Each firm, when deciding upon its pricing and other market strategies, must explicitly take into account the likely reactions of its competitors. (...when it is deciding...)

My patients, if given the opportunity, would freely converse about their problems whilst sitting in my waiting room. (...if they were given...; ...whilst they were sitting...)

She wanted to sleep, if possible. (...if that was possible.)

His working life, although not unstructured, allowed him a kind of freedom. (...although it was not unstructured...)

4.25 Sometimes, in non-finite clauses containing an '-ing'-participle, we have to understand a simple, rather than a continuous, tense.

He described that prospect as 'unlikely', although accepting that any signs of recovery were weak. (...although he accepted...)

Peterson, after having looked the plan over, said, 'Fine, why don't we let Kim try it in his region?' (...after he had looked...)

Before leaving, he asked Sam for an account of his movements during the previous afternoon. (Before he left...)

Without conjunctions

4.26 Some non-finite clauses and verbless clauses have no conjunction. Since such clauses do not contain linking words, this book is not, strictly speaking, the place to discuss them in detail. However, a few points may be noted.

4.27 A non-finite clause which follows a preceding noun or noun group may have a similar function to a relative clause.

A person standing very close to the fire receives more heat than someone standing further away. (...who is standing...)

He took out a folder containing my proposal and slammed it on his desk. (...which contained my proposal...)

We wish you every success in maintaining the high standard of journalism set by your magazine. (...which has been set by your magazine.)

A clause of this kind is sometimes referred to as a ***reduced relative clause***.

4.28 In some non-finite and verbless clauses, you can sometimes understand a meaning of time, reason, or condition. However, without an actual conjunction it is not always clear which meaning is intended. In fact sometimes it may not be clear whether one of these meanings is intended or whether the clause should be interpreted as a reduced relative clause.

Looking out of the window, Holly said, 'You're usually in the shower by this time.' (While she was looking out of the window...)

Cassandra sat down, not wanting to get in his way. (...because she did not want...)

Not having encountered an atlas before, she could not make head or tail of maps. (Because she had not encountered an atlas before...)

Overcome with emotion, Irena burst into Polish. (Because she was overcome...)

Unhappy, not wanting to see more, she went back to Seymour House. (Because she was unhappy and didn't want...)

It had been easy for me to avoid the issue, but now, faced with the man himself, it was impossible to dissemble. ('...when I was faced...' or '...because I was faced...')

Given time, these questions will answer themselves. (Provided that we/you/they are given enough time...)

The will of the people, inspired by God's holy truth, must prevail. ('...because it is inspired by...' or '...when it is inspired by...' or '...if it is inspired by...' or '...which is inspired by...')

4.29 An '-ing'-clause, in some contexts, can mean a result, what happened next.

Both machines crashed near Hatfield, killing their crews.

These developments will lead to local monopolies, leaving customers with less real choice.

'To'-infinitive clauses

4.30 'To'-infinitive clauses have various functions. Often they have a meaning of purpose (see **2.64**), and some are used as connectors – e.g. 'to start with', 'to sum up' (see **3.22, 3.26**).

A 'to'-infinitive clause can have a 'subject' at the beginning of it, introduced by the preposition 'for'.

For me to question you about your homeland goes contrary to all the laws of honour.

For the attack to succeed, surprise was essential.

'To'-infinitive clauses sometimes have a meaning of consequence, something that followed some other action.

I arrived to find the hotel officially closed.

He took his washing machine in for repair, only to be told it needed replacing.

Clauses beginning with prepositions

4.31 Some non-finite and verbless clauses are introduced by prepositions. Clauses of this kind, and the different prepositions that can be used, are discussed in paragraphs **4.32–4.37**.

by, in, on

4.32 These prepositions can be followed by '-ing'-clauses.

By indicates method or manner.

Appointments may be made by calling 414 6203 on weekdays.

By learning how the mind works, scientists hope to construct better computers and software.

By staying in this room you have become a carrier of the illness.

In can suggest a mixture of time and cause.

I believe I am right in saying that I have rather a large influence over a good many people my own age. (...when I say...)

Even the foul weather and my illness couldn't totally account for my disappointment in returning to a holiday destination I remembered fondly. (...when I returned...)

All agree however that the company has been irresponsible in refusing to discuss the issue. (...because they are refusing...)

On followed by an '-ing'-clause means 'when'.

She had a mild attack of hysteria on reaching Jamaica, when she realized her mother had actually died. (...when she reached...)

Their faces lit up on hearing their own language.

He arrived, but, on hearing what the crime was, he turned round instantly and left.

despite, in spite of

4.33 **Despite** and **in spite of** denote concession, and correspond roughly to the conjunction 'although'.

Being the first child meant that she was given the conventional male education despite being a girl.

None of our players is taking anything for granted, despite starting hot favourites.

Corbett helped himself liberally, despite having already eaten.

In spite of getting better for a while, when April came along, her appetite disappeared and by the end of April she was dead.

The Duchess is very active in spite of not having been in particularly good health of late.

See also **2.61**.

without, with

4.34 **Without** followed by an '-ing'-clause means that something is not the case or does not happen.

Without looking up at me, he said, 'Why did your friend go to the museum?'

I would never go to bed without locking my door. (i.e. I always lock the door before I go to bed.)

Julius, I can't keep using your phone without paying for it.

Without wishing to be unkind, she's not the most interesting company. (I don't wish to be unkind, but I think she is not...)

4.35 **With** and **without** often introduce non-finite and verbless adverbial clauses that contain their own subjects. These clauses describe the circumstances in which the events of the main clause happen (or do not happen).

Expenses should be cut by at least 10 per cent, with most savings coming from reduced fees to brokers.

With the door shut and the air-conditioning on, it was almost as though we were locked into some mysterious space capsule.

With Habib away, Hassan's attitude seemed to have changed.

One man was taken away with blood pouring down his face.

She is slumped in her chair with her hands folded between her knees.

I'm going to eat it and enjoy it without you staring down on me like an old sheep.

She wants to do that without them knowing she helped.

I'd be lost without you here.

Note: sometimes a possessive form is used instead of an object noun or pronoun. This usage is nowadays considered rather old-fashioned or formal.

With my getting back so late, we haven't had time to go over the timetables.

Travis had joined them, without Larry's spotting his approach.

She did not understand why she could not say anything without its being interpreted as a sign of madness.

with all

4.36 Clauses beginning **with all**, followed by a noun or noun group, can express reason or concession.

With all the rush, I'd failed to fasten the top strap correctly. (Because of all the rush...)

With all her advantages, she was nowhere near an equal match for him. (Despite her advantages...)

Japan, with all its uniqueness, still has to find its place in the international order which we are trying to build.

for all

4.37 **For all** followed by a noun group can have a meaning of concession ('despite'), or it can suggest that something is unimportant or unsuccessful.

For all his ultra-Irish name, he looked Australian. (Despite his name...)

For all his jokes and laughter he was a dangerous and ambitious man. (Despite his jokes and laughter...)

I ran back for a gun and searched the woods, for all the good it did me. (i.e. It did me no good.)

For all followed by a clause such as 'I care' or 'I know' implies the opposite ('I don't care', 'I don't know').

You can go right now, for all I care.

Everybody's nervous the first day on a job, she assured herself. For all she knew, that was true. (i.e. She didn't know; it might have been true.)

For all we know he may have been in the drug business for years.

Absolute clauses

4.38 Non-finite clauses that lack any subordinating conjunction and that contain their own subjects are called absolute clauses. Sometimes the clause describes the circumstances in which something happens or exists (compare **4.35**). In fact, in the following examples 'with' could be inserted at the beginning of the highlighted clause, without any change of meaning.

I could see her standing on the sidewalk, blood running down her neck.

He ordered Gough to carry out rigorous inspections of cavalry divisions, the aim being to prepare them for the role set forth in the memorandum.

The Captain was bent over the radar, his eyes glued to the scanner.

4.39 Sometimes the meaning of an absolute clause suggests condition ('if', 'provided that'). Absolute clauses of this kind are often idioms or fixed expressions, as in the examples below:

You and your circumstances may well change. That being so, what was right for one time may no longer be right for you now. (If that is so...; If you and your circumstances change...)

Other things being equal, most hostel tenants would prefer single to shared rooms. (Provided that there are not other circumstances that could affect their decisions...)

A helicopter would pick up the two yachtsmen, weather permitting. (...provided that the weather was good enough.)

From now until November, when, God willing, the rains will come, I shall be in the Luangwa valley in Zambia.

5 Reference: pronouns and other pro-forms

5.1 Both in writing and speaking you often want to refer back to something that has already been mentioned. (Occasionally you may also want to point forwards to something you are going to mention.) There are various ways you can do this without repeating yourself. The words you use are not, strictly speaking, 'linking words' (as, for example, connectors are); but they function to make connections and to avoid repetition, sometimes of single words, sometimes of whole clauses.

Pronouns in particular are used in this way, often substituting for a noun or noun group but sometimes substituting for a whole clause. In addition, some determiners, adjectives, adverbs, nouns, and verbs are also used in various types of reference and substitution. One of the commonest ways of referring back is to use 'the', followed by a noun or noun group, to refer to someone or something already mentioned (although 'the', of course, has many other uses).

> *He had an advance from HarperCollins to do a book. If he wasn't going to do the book right away, he'd have to pay the advance back.*

Personal pronouns and determiners

5.2 One common way of referring back (or forwards) to someone or something – whether in the same sentence or an earlier sentence – is by the use of personal pronouns and possessive forms (e.g. 'she', 'her', 'hers', 'it', 'they', 'them', 'their').

> *At the beginning of his working life Taggart had joined a training scheme run by the BBC, and there he had met Jane.* (Note that 'his' refers forward, and 'he' refers back.)

> *In her fright Rosetta seized Gabriel's hand, he felt her plump, soft palm, and entwined his fingers with hers. Gabriel's hand was cold and rough and it pressed hard, harder all the time.*

> *Brand, surprised and none too warm, reluctantly indicated he had no objection. After all he was a guest. Normally it was a haven of peace tucked away in the hills above Salzburg. But not today. When they returned they would find it in the same immaculate order in which they had left it.* (Obviously, 'he' is Brand. But it is not clear what 'it' and 'they' are referring to; 'it' may be a house. Here we have pronouns referring back to something and some people identified in an earlier sentence.)

Quantity pronouns and determiners

5.3 ***Quantity pronouns*** and ***determiners*** (e.g. 'another', 'both', 'neither', 'many', and numbers) can substitute for noun groups referring to people or things. These words can be used without a following noun if the noun (or noun group) they refer to is mentioned elsewhere in the text, so this usage is in fact a form of ellipsis. Here are some examples:

Had he found the gold or the dead man, or both?

She began to consult doctors, and each had a different diagnosis.

Thousands of new diets are dreamed up yearly; many are soon forgotten, a few are sufficiently effective to become popular.

The most startling thing about Goa are the four great Catholic churches built in old Goa and now surrounded by jungle; two had been abandoned to nature but two were still in use.

She was seventy years old but everyone thought she'd last another ten.

Demonstratives

5.4 The ***demonstratives*** ('this', 'that', 'these', and 'those') also work in a similar way, with ellipsis of words that are present elsewhere in the text.

In this and the final chapter we look more closely at the way home ownership has changed. ('this' = 'this chapter'.)

For that and other reasons, the conviction was unsatisfactory. ('that' = 'that reason'.)

People are beginning to realise the true scale of the problems facing them. Some of these are Germany's alone, though with powerful European side-effects. ('these' = 'these problems'.)

She told me she loved me more than all my brothers and sisters combined. She was afraid to show it because they would be jealous. Those were her exact words. ('those' = 'those words'.)

5.5 Demonstratives can also substitute in a more general way, but normally for things, not people.

The cost of the operation in 1990 and 1991 will be nearly 10 million dollars. Over half of this relates to personnel costs such as salaries, fees and travel expenses.

A century earlier, Messina had had a famous architectural seafront, lined with elegant palaces. Only remnants of that remained now.

An alternative to cash is investment in Government bonds, also known as gilts. These represent money borrowed by the government to finance its Public Sector Borrowing Requirement.

I'm quite happy if you ignore the format of the essay and just produce a sheet in which you say 'These are my thoughts'.

Rights? You ceased to have those from the moment you were brought here.

Clements put three packets of ammunition on the arm of Malone's chair. 'We found those in a steel box in the garage.'

5.6 However, 'those' can sometimes refer to people, but only with a word or phrase added. This is still the case even if there is a noun or noun group to which the word refers back.

Yes, you can trust a botanist; at least, those from the Royal Botanic Gardens.

The public is only interested in generals who win battles, not in those who lose them.

Substitution: 'one', 'ones'

5.7 The pronoun **one** can substitute for a singular count noun, and **ones** for a plural noun. 'One' can stand alone, but 'ones' needs another word or phrase to modify it.

I have an aspirin, if you want one.

Imagine a doll that has your face and is your doll! Everyone will want one. (i.e. a doll with its owner's face.)

The green light went out, the red one came on.

The top front teeth are the ones which are most at risk from tooth decay.

Who are your favorite tennis players? Who are the ones that when you watch a championship you're hoping will win?

He is one of those actors who has made a lot of films but few good ones.

5.8 Notice that 'one' and 'ones' in contexts of this sort are primarily substitutes for other words, whereas 'it' and 'them' refer directly to things in the 'real world'.

Merely having enough houses for the number of families that claim to want one would not remove the housing problem. ('one' = a house of some kind.)

The house is in the hands of the agents, but until it's sold it's yours to use if you want it. ('it' = that particular house.)

Notice also the difference between 'it' and 'one' in the following example:

He felt he had to tear off the label and replace it with an identical one.

5.9 Sometimes several different pronouns all refer back to something mentioned earlier.

Small meteorites hit the Earth all the time. Most of them incinerate in the atmosphere. The cores of the larger ones survived to pulverise craters on the earth; many of them have been eroded or obliterated by glaciation, but some have survived. Others have landed in the deep Antarctic ice: they are regularly retrieved and studied because they are less likely to be contaminated with earth material. Some come from outside the solar system, a few are believed to have come from Mars.

All the highlighted pronouns in the above passage refer in some way to meteorites which reach the earth. However, as the paragraph proceeds, the specific reference of the pronouns changes as follows: small meteorites ('them'), meteorites in general ('ones'), the larger meteorites ('them', 'some'), meteorites in general again ('others'), the meteorites in the Antarctic ice ('they', 'they'), and then back once more to meteorites in general ('some', 'a few').

Referring to place and time

here, there

5.10 The adverbs **here** and **there** can be used as ***pro-forms*** to refer to places mentioned or implied elsewhere in the text. Of course, in conversation, the meaning of 'here' is often understood from the context, as the place where the conversation is taking place; no other reference is needed.

The house stood near a quiet sandy beach facing across the vast distances of the Lake of Oulu; here she could wander and imagine herself on the edge of a great sea.

His first call had been at his lawyers. Here he had learnt that none of the cases had been decided one way or another.

Soon, he was on Adalbertstrasse. Number eighty-four would be less than a five-minute walk. Here was the worst bomb damage he had seen.

My father expects to land at Portsmouth within the fortnight. It would mean so much to me to be there on the dock, waiting for him.

Dad's at the hospital with Sam. The police are going to take us there.

now, then

5.11 **Now** and **then** can be used in a similar way to 'here' and 'there', as pro-forms of time. Although 'now', in conversation, usually refers to the present time, this is not always the case in writing: it can be used to talk about the past, with the meaning 'at that same time', a time already mentioned or implied.

They told her it was the rainy season now where Peter was (the time when the snakes are most active, she recalled.)

Through the telescope the hunter saw Sementsev move foward. Now he was the perfect target.

Sharpe looked behind again and saw his closest pursuers were now just fifty yards away.

From 1985-90 I was an instructor at the regional party headquarters. After that I went back to work in a factory. Then I had no idea what a casino was.

We left just after one-thirty. By then the wind had risen almost to gale force.

Substitution for clauses

this, that, it

5.12 Certain pronouns, notably **this**, **that**, and **it**, can be substituted for previous clauses or sections of text. The substitution is not necessarily word for word – we understand the meaning and adjust the words slightly. In the examples below, the highlighted parts show what the pronoun is referring back to.

He employed a housekeeper about whom he would sometimes remark, rather unkindly, that not only was she of indeterminate age, but also of indeterminate sex, unaware that this was exactly what others frequently said about him.

They had thought that they might climb out under the cover of darkness. It only took a few minutes to discover that this was impossible.

Upon its introduction to Europe coffee was hailed as an aphrodisiac, which made it very popular. It was perhaps with this in mind that Voltaire drank sixty cups a day.

We lived together, off and on, for two years. This was way before that was an acceptable thing to do. ('this' = our living together; 'that' = any couple living together.)

'I wonder if the police have managed to get hold of Matt. I'll try and find out,' Brand assured her. 'That would be a relief,' she said gratefully.

At first I thought that this reorganization was simply an attempt on his part to gain more power. But that is not the explanation.

'I'm so lonely.' I said it aloud, trying to mean it, trying to feel the ache.

They go to motor racing to watch cars crash, but it's a pretty unattractive thought.

5.13 'This' (but not 'that') and 'it' can refer forward to text.

I hate to say this but I don't think they're kidding.

I know him better than any of you, and I can say this: nobody's going to make him work any faster.

Well, I'm ashamed to say it, but I don't care for my war duties at all.

so, not

5.14 **So** and **not** can refer back and substitute for clauses, particularly after reporting verbs, and after expressions such as 'I'm afraid', 'it appears', and 'it seems'.

They hated children. I heard them say so. (i.e. that they hated children.)

'Actually, when you see somebody die gradually they go so thin, you know.'—'Yeah, I believe so.'

'But you'll be taken prisoner, won't you?'— 'I hope not.'

'Were there any survivors?'— 'No, sir. I'm afraid not.'

Is he being honest with the people? So far, it appears not.

'How did the accident occur? I assume it was an accident.'—'It seems so.'

'So' and 'not' also substitute for clauses in the expressions 'if so', 'if not', and 'even so'. See also **2.40**, **2.53**.

Did Rose have a passport? And if so, where was it?

Ask her if it is a convenient time. If not, can she suggest another possible time?

Iris avoided wine with her meal but even so she felt unutterably drowsy afterwards.

5.15 'So', and especially 'not', are also used as clause substitutes after 'perhaps', 'probably', 'maybe', and 'possibly'.

'I am sure he would tell you were you to ask him.'—'Perhaps so, but I do not wish to risk a snub.'

Perhaps this time we will make a better job of it. Or perhaps not.

'Does it matter?'—'No, probably not,' said Irena.

'You're probably better equipped to do it than he would be even if he were here.'—'Maybe so. But it's hard all the same.'

Maybe the police would believe it, maybe not.

'I don't know any secrets.'—'Possibly not. But it's more probable that you do know some but haven't recognized their value.'

5.16 'So' as a clause-substitute is sometimes used emphatically as the first word in a clause or sentence. This happens mainly with verbs of thinking and saying (i.e. reporting verbs).

It's an example of Victorian architecture, so I've been told.

'Everything about him was well documented.'—'So I believe.'

Clauses of this kind often suggest an element of doubt or disbelief about the truth of the previous clause.

'He made a genuine mistake.'—'Yeah, so he says.'

Choosing which type of greenhouse was a simple task; or so I thought.

Nothing changes, or so it seems.

Substitution using 'do'

5.17 **Do so, do it**, and **do that** can substitute for a predicate (i.e. a whole clause minus its subject.) Tenses may be changed in the substitution.

He tried to remember where he might have seen her before, but could not do so. (...but could not remember.)

I always read a lot and I am doing so more than ever while preparing a new TV programme. (...and I am reading more than ever...)

She nearly died at the age of 95 in June, and finally did so in July.

Faraday made a note in his diary in 1822: 'Convert magnetism into electricity!' It was 1831 before he did so, and what a revolution it caused. (...before he converted magnetism into electricity...)

We can make a difference in the world in which we live. We can do it because we believe in the power and the spirit of our own will.

Now we'll go and talk to your mother. Don't you want to do that?

General nouns used for reference

5.18 A common way of referring back to another noun (or noun group) is to use a noun combined with a determiner such as 'the', 'this', or 'such'. Sometimes the same noun is repeated, but often a synonym (another word with roughly the same meaning) is used, or a more general word that includes the meaning of the other word. For example, the word 'child' can include the word 'daughter'. Sometimes a word is used that belongs to the same area of meaning, based on our knowledge of the real world. For example, in the second example below, we know that if we combine mayonnaise and mashed potatoes, the result is a mixture.

Beside her slept her two-year-old daughter, Belle. The child's forehead was damp with perspiration.

Combine the thick garlic mayonnaise with the mashed potatoes and spread this mixture on rounds of toasted French bread.

Some very general nouns are regularly used to refer (backwards or forwards), not only to other nouns, but also, for example, to sentences describing actions, events, ideas, or statements.

thing, case, way

5.19 Among the commonest of these general nouns is **thing**. This can be substituted for a noun referring to an object.

He brought out the compass which he'd removed from the lifeboat. 'This thing's virtually useless, but at least it does show changes in direction.'

More importantly, 'thing' can refer to something such as an idea, action, event, or situation.

Trying to avoid or minimize risk, however, is not the same thing as trying to eliminate it.

Infection and inflammation are not exactly the same thing.

Why is it that feminists always say 'women feel' when what they mean is 'feminists feel'? It is not at all the same thing. (i.e. These two statements do not express the same idea.)

I coerced Ray, who wasn't religious at all, to attend the church with me and convert, which was a big mistake, because the next thing I knew, he'd become a fanatic.

The thing I like about Wallace is that he is not worried about failure.

Another very general noun is **case**, referring to an event, situation, or circumstance.

Some visitors may come by road from Zaire; in that case, they will probably enter Zambia through Kaumbalesa or Mokambo.

You'll be a lawyer or a policeman, and in either case, your studies will stand you in good stead.

Way can refer to the means or method by which something is done.

If an unemployed worker refuses training or a job his benefits are stopped. In this way, Sweden has virtually abolished long-term unemployment.

We have decided to use the jam you sent us only with our evening cup of tea, and in that way it will last us a long time.

Some examples of other general nouns can be seen in the following paragraphs. For a fuller discussion of nouns which are used to refer backwards and forwards, see Chapter 6.

Uses of 'such'

5.20 The determiner and pronoun 'such', as a 'referring back' word, is used in two main ways:

- Firstly, it can combine with other words as part of a noun group to mean things, people, or actions 'like that', 'of that sort'.

- Secondly, it is used in the expression 'as such', meaning 'in the exact sense of the preceding word or phrase'.

Such (with or without an adjective) is used before singular and plural count nouns, and before uncount nouns.

There have long been rumours that they have been trying to acquire anti-aircraft missiles, but this is the first time they have claimed the use of such a weapon. (i.e. an anti-aircraft missile.)

He had never seen a woman in his close family openly lose her temper with a male relative, and believed that only bad women did such a thing. (i.e. lose their temper with a male relative.)

He is quite ambitious and is prepared to work hard. Such people should be given a chance to get on. (i.e. people who are ambitious and prepared to work hard.)

Ultimately developing countries would like to be able to generate their own technology. In the interim, such countries must depend primarily on imports.

He cheerfully travelled economy class, even though his height was beginning to make such cramped conditions uncomfortable. (i.e. the sort of cramped conditions that are typical of economy class.)

Their experimental method gives rise to accusations of bias. But such 'bias' cannot be wholly explained as the product of personal views of staff members.

My friends would take the children out and keep them for a night to give me a break. And my doctor continued to listen, to believe, teaching me how to cope. I was very lucky to be surrounded by such understanding and love. (i.e. the understanding and love shown to me by my friends and my doctor.)

5.21 **Such** can also follow 'all', 'any', 'many', 'no', 'one', and 'some', occasionally without a following noun.

All social theories are designed to either advance the science of society or to promote fraudulent ideas concerning society. Thus, all such theories are developed with some use in mind.

She had threatened to inform London that she could no longer take responsibility for working with me. I warned her against any such course. (course = course of action.)

Marcia recognized the evening as one which Robert had decided not to enjoy. There were many such. (... many evenings like that.)

'I'll tell you what I'll do, catch the first plane back to Los Angeles.' Even as she said it she knew she would do no such thing. (...she would not catch a plane back to L.A.)

'I just want justice.'—'There's no such thing any more and you're not being honest. You want revenge.'

Festivals often had huge orchestras. In the T'ang dynasty one such had 120 harpists alone. (...one huge orchestra...)

Anthony, darling, is one of us about to say that this is stronger than us, or some such nonsense? (...some similarly absurd statement.)

He personally hoped that the Nature Conservancy or some such body would buy up the island. (...some similar organization.)

as such

5.22 **As such** refers back to the immediately preceding word or phrase and means 'in the exact sense of the term'.

He had no plan of action as such. (i.e. He had no actual plan, though perhaps he had various ideas about what to do.)

The note was a blatant attempt to evade mail censorship and as such was against prison regulations.

Escaping prisoners of war could expect to be treated as such. Unidentified strangers masquerading as foreign workmen could expect to be dealt with as spies.

5.23 Note: 'so' can sometimes substitute for a previously mentioned adjective.

I found the street where Eddie lived. It was narrow, made more so by the cars parked on both sides. (...made narrower by...)

As a complement (e.g. with the verb 'be'), 'so' is often placed at the beginning of a clause for emphasis, with subject-auxiliary inversion. Compare **5.16**.

Gwendolen, you're crazy. I know, and so are you. (...and you are crazy too)

Life is great. So are you, and the flowers aren't really enough to express it.

Such is occasionally fronted in a similar way.

She was struck by a picture of a woman with a long dress and a plunging neckline and a tall hair-do. Such were the fashions in those days. (i.e. That is what the fashions were in those days.)

Uses of 'sort', 'kind', and 'type'

this sort/kind/type, that sort/kind/type

5.24 One way of saying that something is like (or not like) something mentioned earlier is to use phrases such as these, usually linked to a particular noun by a following or preceding 'of'. So, 'that kind of book' means more or less the same as 'a book of that kind'.

I have played a lot of glamorous women who have broken men's hearts, so people tend to see me as that sort of person.

We often blame ourselves for things that happen to other people. That kind of belief is not at all unusual.

So now this has been definitely diagnosed as the Plague. There has been consternation everywhere, because when this sort of disease is brought into a country there is no knowing how far it will spread.

We ended up teaching mainly foreigners, teachers, journalists and people of of that kind.

Many 'scientific' journals have a disgraceful attitude to parapsychology and completely reject and suppress any publications of that type.

5.25 Phrases such as 'this type of thing' and 'that kind of thing' are very common, with 'thing' often meaning an action or event, rather than a concrete object.

They heckled him, and threw things. Quite nasty, but of course if you're a minister these days, with current standards of behaviour, you have to get used to that sort of thing.

He was not suited to the role of detective: there were professionals who did this sort of thing, and did it far more efficiently.

Some of them are drinking beer, partying late at night, that kind of thing.

People keep asking me to do things. Reviews, articles, that kind of thing.

It is specially important to guard against accidents. All good parents have fire-guards and gates at dangerous places, but I strongly advise you to get this kind of thing thoroughly organized some time before it actually seems necessary.

'What sort of bother?'— 'Well, running off without paying and that type of thing.'

5.26 Particularly in spoken English, you may hear 'these' and 'those' used before 'sort of', 'kind of', and 'type of' followed by a plural noun, although 'sort', 'kind', and 'type' themselves are in the singular. However, many people regard this usage as ungrammatical, so it tends to be avoided in writing.

I was asking her what it was like, you know, I mean, what's your weather like and all these sort of boring questions.

People like us shouldn't work these kind of hours.

He is very good-looking if you like those sort of looks.

That way we don't have to provide the showers, the food services, the washers and dryers, those type of things.

Comparative forms

5.27 A comparison must, by definition, be between at least two people, things, or ideas, so comparative forms (including 'another' and 'other') always refer to someone or something else in some way. Sometimes that second person or thing may be implied by the situation or context, and need not necessarily have been previously expressed in words.

Can I have another coffee?

Where's the other sock?

5.28 Often a comparison points forwards, that is, the standard of comparison occurs later in the sentence than the comparative adjective or adverb and the thing, person, or action which it describes. In these cases, the standard of comparison is introduced by **than** (or **as** if it is a comparison of equality). See also **2.84–2.87**.

The latest earthquakes are smaller than the one which shook the area on Sunday.

We must move to accept the idea that two parents and one or two children are an easier equation than one parent and one or two children.

Some words tend to occur more often than others.

I hope I look as good as you when I'm your age.

Elsewhere, comparative forms are another way of referring back to something already mentioned, or possibly merely implied.

This is a junior school. You'll go to a bigger one for girls of your age.

There are probably about a thousand Americans, and a lot of other nationalities, in smaller numbers.

They should visit the North West where everything is cheaper.

Some broken bones heal quickly and some more slowly.

Make the music hearable, both to the people in the audience and, just as important, to the onstage musicians themselves.

the former, the latter

5.29 When you are referring back to two different things or people and you are comparing them in some way, you can refer to what you mentioned first as **the former** and what you mentioned second as **the latter**. These are fairly formal phrases, but they occur in speech as well as in writing. A noun can be added.

There are rules which govern not only the working lives of our nurses, but also their off-duty lives. While I demand adherence to the former, I am, I hope, sufficiently realistic to realize that the latter are mostly out-of-date.

You know what Democritus said on the subject. 'Do not trust all men, but trust men of worth.' The former course is silly, the latter a mark of prudence.

I couldn't tell if he was being careless and unstructured, or if he was a clever interrogator. I was beginning to suspect the latter.

The same or different?

the same, the opposite, the reverse

5.30 'Same', 'opposite', and 'reverse' are adjectives with no comparative forms but essentially their meaning involves comparing one thing with another.

You can use **the same**, **the opposite** and, more rarely, **the reverse** to refer back to an event, idea, or chunk of text. You can use a verb in front of them if necessary. You can also enlarge these expressions to include a noun.

Their questions were clear and concise. The same could not be said for the answers. (i.e. The answers were not clear and concise.)

I have a friend who went to France as a male au pair without any trouble. I do not see why I cannot do the same here. (i.e. be a male au pair.)

'Do you enjoy your job?'—'I could ask you the same.'

His coldness angered her. She had made her impulsive offer in a spirit of straightforward friendliness, and she wanted him to accept it in the same way.

Morris has played well in both matches and I would say the same thing for Andrews.

She realized that compared with most women she was remarkably inexperienced in this sort of thing. What worried her more than anything else was that Mike might think exactly the opposite. (i.e. that she was experienced.)

He remained silent, resisting the impulse to encourage Stephen to talk, which he knew might well have the opposite effect.

I hope that anything I report will have the effect of being useful to our purpose, not the reverse.

The interview had not reassured Tweed. Rather the reverse. (i.e. It had worried him.)

ee also **at the same time: 2.60.**

ikewise, otherwise

.31 Likewise and **otherwise** always refer back. In Chapters 2 and 3, here are examples showing them as connectors, standing somewhat part from their sentences. They can also follow a verb. **Do likewise** is nother possible way of saying 'do the same', 'act in the same way'.

The boy and his mother emerged from the next-door house, got into their respective cars, and drove away. As soon as they were out of sight, Bernard did likewise. (i.e. got into his car.)

He put family honour above all else, and taught us to do likewise.

therwise is particularly used after 'do' and after some verbs with a eneral 'thinking' meaning (e.g. 'decide', 'know', 'pretend', 'prove', uggest'). It means 'differently' or 'the opposite'.

He pleaded guilty in spite of considerable pressure to do otherwise.

You should still continue your course of these drugs to prevent the infection recurring, unless your doctor advises otherwise.

He was hurt and it was no use pretending otherwise.

'Do you think she really is what she says?'—'I think she is sure that there is nothing we can do to prove otherwise'.

dentical, similar, different

.32 These adjectives all compare two or more people or things. As ith ordinary comparative forms, the comparison can point forwards r backwards (see **5.28**). When it points forwards, each of the three djectives has a characteristic preposition (or prepositions) linking it the standard of comparison. The related adverbs 'identically', imilarly', and 'differently' are also sometimes used in this way.

you say something is **identical to** or **with** something else, you are saying either that it is exactly the same or that it is very much like it. Identical twins are usually difficult to tell apart!

I joined a group of women dressed in turquoise sweatsuits identical to mine.

I was very reluctant to accept that robots were identical with human beings.

It would be easy to produce a balanced composition by echoing a line on the left side of the painting with an identical line on the right.

Cobuild appears to have been confused with an identically named company based in Greater Manchester.

Things or people that are not quite identical may be described a **similar to** each other. For the use of 'similarly' as a connector, se **3.11**.

The accident was similar to one that happened in 1973.

Place the almond and coconut oils together in a double saucepan or similar utensil over a low heat.

These theories of brain function sound less compelling when you learn that in the 19th century a similar argument raged about the function of the lobes of the brain. (Notice that 'argument' is being used as a near synonym of 'theory'.)

Germany's diplomatic service is structured similarly to that of Britain.

'I'm so sorry,' I muttered, or something similarly inadequate.

By contrast, you can describe things or people that are unlike others a **different from** them.

London was different from most European capitals.

The figures suggest that the company is surviving the recession better than most, but the second half may tell a different story.

They still get treated differently from almost every other contemporary British band.

What had begun as a command ended up quite differently; it came as close as John could get to a threat.

Different to and **different than** (which is predominantly a American usage) are also used, though some speakers consider tha only 'different from' is correct.

Soya beans are quite different to any other bean in flavour and texture.

We have a different relationship with horses than we do with cattle and sheep and pigs.

Notice that 'different than' is useful when introducing a clause. If determined to use 'from' in the last example above, a speaker would have to say something awkward like 'a different relationship from the kind we have with cattle, sheep, and pigs'.

5.33 Note: **differently** sometimes functions almost like the object of a verb, with a meaning rather like 'the opposite' or 'otherwise'.

> *She had started the business and had come to believe it would fail without her. The last few months had taught her differently. The company was thriving in her absence.*
>
> *Until now I thought that this sort of accident was the owner's fault but now I know differently.*

equal, additional

5.34 Both **equal** (and **equally**) and **additional** can refer back. If you say something is equal to something else you mean it is the same in size or value etc, that it shares some characteristic with something else 'to the same extent'.

> *Each Christmas Anthony sent him carefully chosen and expensive presents. He received letters of gratitude composed with equal care.* (i.e. with as much care as the care taken in choosing the presents.)
>
> *She was not used to making apologies and she was equally nervous about developing relationships.*
>
> *Nick was already nursing a grudge against her because of what happened this morning. She did not want to give him any additional cause for grievance.* (The first cause was 'what happened this morning'.)

For the use of 'equally' and 'additionally' as connectors, see **3.12** and **3.4**.

Written conventions

5.35 All the words and phrases already dealt with in this chapter can, of course, be used in both speech and writing. But there are several words and phrases that are particularly used by writers when referring to some other part of their text.

as we have seen, as we saw (earlier), as we shall see

5.36 Sometimes to call their readers' attention to the fact that they are referring to their text, writers use phrases like **as we have seen** or

as we shall see. They may or may not add another word such as 'earlier' or 'later'.

As we have seen, the increase in the prison population is due to an increase in long-term sentences.

As we saw earlier, the evidence of the past is hard to read, but easy to interpret wrongly.

For this reason, as we saw in Part Two, a fat such as butter is better to cook with than sunflower oil.

The acquisition of this technology places a great burden on the foreign currency resources of the underdeveloped countries, although as we shall see later on this may be lessened by various forms of aid.

above, below

5.37 **Above** and **below** are used exclusively in writing, and usually refer to earlier or later text in the same chapter.

As we saw above in the section on product quality and service, the customer will pay more readily if the product and service match expectations.

The numerical symbols in the Index (pages 2-3) are explained below.

as follows, the following

5.38 **As follows** and **the following** are also virtually written conventions only. They are immediately followed by whatever list or explanation is intended. A noun can be added to 'the following'.

Prepare a mayonnaise sauce as follows: In a bowl place egg yolks, mustard, salt and pepper. Pour the oil in gradually while beating with a whisk.

The question at issue is the following: what does scientific criticism of ideals and value-judgements mean and what is its purpose?

Please therefore place in the Boston Globe automobile classified advertising section the following notice: 'WANTED: Blue Mercedes Benz'.

The orders for a trip to Italy included the following instructions: All players will report to the Great Western Railway Hotel, Paddington, London, in time for dinner early on Saturday evening.

chapter, section

5.39 Writers who wish to refer readers back or forwards to another part of their book can mention another chapter or section.

We saw in a previous chapter that audio tapes playing suitable music can be very useful as preparation for meditation.

As we've already discussed in an earlier chapter, we warm more to people who we assume are similar to ourselves than to those who don't appear to be.

We shall see in the next chapter that language plays an exceedingly important part in the process of memory.

As was noted in the previous section, policies of prevention and community care in all the services led to a renewed interest in family welfare.

The next section looks at the causes of stress in more detail.

Notice in these examples various alternatives to 'as we saw', 'as we have seen' or 'as we shall see'.

the last chapter

5.40 Theoretically **the last chapter** is ambiguous, since it could mean either 'the previous chapter to this' or 'the final chapter of the book'. In practice when a writer is referring to his or her own text, it almost always refers back to the previous chapter, as tenses make clear.

As we have seen in the last chapter, competitive, pluralistic politics is likely to mean that a wide variety of points of view and interests is brought to bear on matters of urban development.

In the last chapter we looked briefly at the idea that language acquisition is partly genetic and partly the result of experience.

As we noted in the last chapter, one of the key ingredients of the official line has been opposition to communism.

6 Reference: nouns

6.1 Chapter 5 contains a number of examples of general nouns being used to refer back to pieces of text describing actions, events, ideas, statements, and so on. The words discussed include 'thing', 'case', and 'way'. Such words are not linking words in a strict grammatical sense; their use is primarily semantic, based on meaning, but when they are used in this general way they are usually used with a determiner such as 'the' or 'this'. So, by indicating links, they help to bind sentences together into a text, something we understand as a piece of language, rather than as a random collection of unrelated sentences.

We shall now go on to discuss a greater range of these general nouns. Notice, firstly, that the nouns are usually used with some sort of determiner, and secondly, that, although in most of the examples in this chapter, these nouns refer back, in some they are referring forwards.

The structure of this chapter is as follows:

- Nouns referring to various kinds of actions, events, and situations: **6.2–6.15**.
- Nouns referring to facts, statements, and ideas: **6.16–6.33**.
- Nouns referring to text as text: **6.34–6.37**.

Actions, events, and situations

6.2 Many words that refer to actions, events, and situations are fairly neutral – you can use them whether you think what happened was good or bad or neither. But some (as indicated below) indicate approval or disapproval.

act, action, activity, course (of action), move, process

6.3 An 'act' and an 'action' are similar, but if you describe something as an **act**, you are probably seeing it as something single and complete, whereas **action** puts more emphasis on the purpose and the process.

> *He decided to put the car away in the garage. He saw this act as something that it was absolutely necessary for him to do at the moment.*
>
> *Finally he cleans all the parts of his bike in the sink so carefully that his granny, who interrupts him in the act, thinks he's doing the dishes.*

The government says environmental taxation will be introduced only when competitor countries take the same action.

The diploma will be duly prepared and, after it has been signed by the proper officers, it will come forward to you by registered post. I hope that this action on our part will afford you a small part of the pleasure which we have received in performing it.

He looked up at the sky, the first action of any person who's been locked away against his will.

US fighters intercepted that plane and forced it to land in Italy. Now, this action was taken at great personal risk to those military personnel.

As for banning a record for being offensive, such actions often have the reverse effect. 'Relax' went straight to number one.

If you talk about (an) **activity**, you are stressing that a lot is happening, that the action is very 'busy'.

If you're a bricklayer or an athlete you will need more food to 'fuel' that activity than if you are a secretary or a student. (i.e. the activity involved in being a bricklayer or an athlete.)

A hospital has many functions to perform, including the prevention and treatment of disease, the education of both health professionals and patients, and the conduct of clinical research. All these activities must be conducted with an overriding concern for the patient.

A **course of action** or a **move** usually refers to a planned action. To refer to a **course** on its own (i.e. without 'of action') is rarer and more formal in this sense.

What he would really have liked to do was dig his garden. However, this course of action was out of the question.

There is little chance that any bank will introduce charges on credit balances this month, or even this year. Such a move would be exploited instantly by its rivals.

Almost all state enterprises should be sold off or closed over the next few months. As with the constitution and decentralisation, these moves create both promise and risk.

As was the custom among Suki's people, her father said nothing to his daughter about his plans for her marriage. Such a course would never have entered his mind. (i.e. the idea of telling her about his plans.)

A **process** is a series of actions, or a continuing action.

These huge trees, in fact, are feeding on themselves, for the moment their leaves fall they decay and become the 'food' on which the trees feed. So rapid is this process that only a thin topsoil is able to form.

He leapt on me and took away the knife, wounding me in the process.

circumstance(s), context, position, situation, state of affairs, state

6.4 Sometimes you want to refer to events or other conditions in which something else happens. These 'background' events or conditions can be referred to by these various general nouns. With 'circumstance', the plural is far more common than the singular. See also **case: 5.19**.

This extra production, combined with a seasonal slump in demand, has caused sharp falls in the prices of some crude oils in recent weeks. Under these circumstances, present market weakness is hardly surprising.

The Nuremberg trials took place in the aftermath of a great war and total surrender. Such circumstances are rare and do not exist in the Bosnian case.

The nurses were all very nice and helpful and assumed that I knew nothing about what would be done. I'm glad they did. In this circumstance I am a patient, not a doctor.

Now at this point two odd circumstances met together. The landlords were, in fact, a religious society of the strictest Protestant principles. That was one circumstance. The other was this: the firm wrote their letter begging for a slight delay on 'Unknown World' letter paper.

Not only did stress literally save our lives, but we almost became addicted to the stress reaction, liking to fight even when not necessary. In this context, modern man's behaviour begins to make sense.

'I'm living on massive bank overdrafts.'—'I understand,' Jefferson murmured, 'I'll help you.'—'No, no,' Mahoney said, I'm just explaining my position.'

Not much is usually said about these students who feel ashamed, embarrassed and failures. Hence it is important to know what can be done for those who find themselves in this position.

The headlines were mostly about the current unrest and the government's inability to get on top of the situation.

I realized one morning that, in the near future, there would only be the two of us at breakfast. The two of us: that state of affairs which I secretly hoped for.

The rest of the children were illegitimate, a very terrible state of affairs in those days.

The only thing that irritated me was that I could not shave. I could feel the stubble on my face, a state of affairs I have always found intolerable.

State often refers to someone's mental, physical, or emotional condition.

Being in an hypnotic trance is rather like being on the borderland between sleep and waking. You feel warm and comfortable and drowsy. While in this state your logical mind fades into the background.

He'd obviously been drinking and he looked flushed and angry. I've never seen him in such a state before or since.

plight, predicament

.5 A **plight** is a difficult, sometimes dangerous, situation to be in.

When her husband died of tuberculosis, she had been turned out of her cottage with her nine-year-old daughter. Walking by chance in a lane close to Oldbury, she met my father and told him of her plight.

Schrader was horrified when he saw the conditions the slum children had to live in. He donates hundreds of thousands of dollars every year to ease their plight.

A **predicament** is similar, but it may be a situation that confronts the person involved with problems, with choices and decisions to be made.

This remarkably sensitive thinker stood at the crossroads of the 'modern' and the 'post-modern', but felt nothing but despair in this predicament.

He realized that the barge had stopped. He knew by the hum of the engine that it was out of gear. He began to worry about his predicament and studied the river bank, hoping to find a place to climb out. There was none.

esult, development, effect, outcome

.6 These are some of the nouns which can be used when various events or states are seen as the result of some other events or actions.

By 1985 the share of manufactures in the exports of these countries was approaching that of industrialized countries. This result should dispel the notion that developing countries are dependent on exports of agricultural products.

During another experiment, though, she saw two images. This result was unexpected but turned out to be extremely important.

Through sheer grit and determination he managed to climb back from 26th to sixth at the finish. 'I could be very pleased with this result later,' he said.

Politically, a Russian military commitment would be a great fillip. But Moscow's leaders seem effectively to have ruled out such a development.

Chemistry was continually advancing knowledge of both the organic and inorganic world. Moreover, many of these developments were directly useful in industry.

Vegetarians have significantly thinner blood and lower blood pressure than meat eaters. This effect is caused partly by a reduction in the number of red blood cells.

The court decided that the time she had already served in prison was sufficient punishment for the manslaughter charge. This outcome could just as easily have occurred with a male defendant.

episode, event, experience

6.7 Something that happens which is important or unusual can be referred to as an **episode**, an **event**, or an **experience**.

If you should remember anything else about that visit of yours to the garage, anything at all, give me a ring. The more you go over the episode in your mind, the more real it will become.

I had to walk a mile and a half before I found a petrol station that had a tow truck. One of the mechanics drove me back to the car, took off the damaged tyre, and took it back to the station to be patched. After it was repaired, he brought it back to the car and put it on. The entire episode took over two-and-a-half hours.

The husband subsequently pleaded guilty to the assault and was convicted. At the time of the event the victim was 38 and had four children.

Of course if you are going to a party, or performing an important public role, that's different. Just make sure your make-up all comes off after the event.

An **experience** stresses the event from the point of view of the person or people involved.

To his surprise, he was met by sullen apathy. The experience disturbed him, he was used to an enthusiastic welcome.

And now came perhaps the worst experience of all – fire. Not fire aboard the ship – that would have been easy to escape – but fire on the surface of the sea.

Occasionally, objects, rather than people, are considered to have had an 'experience'. This usage is rather metaphorical, and is sometimes intended to be humorous.

Most of the furniture had spent the last six months in storage and some of it, she thought, looked a little worse for the experience.

Compare **incident: 6.15**.

manner, method, means, practice, system

6.8 There are several nouns that can refer to the way in which something is done. **Method** suggests that this particular way is intentional and deliberate; **practice** and **system** imply that it is regular or repeated.

My children lay down upon the earth, and in this manner we passed the entire night.

Before killing them, they fire shots in the air in order to attract the attention of people living nearby. In this manner, the soldiers ensure that the executions are witnessed by friends and families of the victims.

Leave the beans to stand for 6-8 hours in a cool place, then drain. The harder the bean, the more it will benefit from longer soaking so this method is advisable for soya beans, chick peas and butter beans especially.

In 1823 acupuncture was mentioned in a leading medical journal and in 1824 Dr Elliotson, a physician at St Thomas's Hospital, London, began to use this method of treatment.

The elite troops should be sent in to attack at whatever point the enemy appeared to be weakened. By this means the decisive attack would come as a surprise.

Where agriculture gave poor returns, people had to search for other means to supplement their diet.

Claude may have done some painting outdoors and certainly Constable did, but the practice was not widespread at this time.

We found that the management was passing discounts in cash to individuals who gave them business. When I found out I gave the management three months to stop the practice.

You may set up a trust fund in which you place cash in trust for whomever you wish. This system avoids the highest levels of taxation and often carries out your instructions well.

A further act of Parliament took the regulation of admissions and detention of mental patients out of legal hands and gave it over to doctors. Most psychiatrists felt that this system worked well.

phenomenon, possibility

6.9 A **phenomenon** is something, often rather strange, that is seen to happen. It is a fairly formal word.

Steve opened his mouth as if to speak, but stopped talking even before he had started. Rose knew that phenomenon. She still saw it daily, as if Steve had words ready to pour out to her and bit them back.

The pilot recalled some difficulty in reading the thermometers, not realizing that he was suffering from an inadequate supply of oxygen. This insidious phenomenon leaves its victim in a state of euphoria, unaware that his physical and mental processes have been seriously affected.

A **possibility** is something that might happen.

'The police may have the car followed and may even have it stopped on some pretext', Rebet persisted. 'I have foreseen that possibility; that is why a second car will follow the first one'

The thyroid gland can either over- or under-function. Either of these possibilities causes a change in the person's psychological functioning as well as in their physical well-being.

achievement, exploit, feat

6.10 All three words here can refer to actions that involve some effort. An **achievement** does not necessarily involve physical force; it may be something like passing an exam or persuading someone else to do something. **Exploits** and **feats** tend to be more physical: a 'feat' often involves considerable difficulty. 'Achievement' and 'feat' are usually words of praise: you can describe some action as an 'exploit' because you think it brave or amusing, but it is possible that you do not approve.

Many famous and successful people have mastered the outward skills of confident behaviour and their very success is a credit to this achievement.

She has now learned to walk about with the help of crutches and stand while resting against chairs or tables. But the numerous scars on her frail, underdeveloped legs bear testimony to the suffering involved in these achievements.

Louis Bleriot flew his light aircraft across the Channel to Dover on 25 July 1909. This achievement ranks alongside that of Lindbergh.

After graduating from high school, having learned nothing except how to put the school paper to press, he joined a friend in canoeing

2,200 miles from Minneapolis to Canada's Hudson Bay. The exploit helped land him a job as a copy boy on the Minneapolis Journal.

Rebels have been operating with a captured fishing boat, and also with coastguard vessels taken from the government. Among their other exploits they managed to hijack a cargo ship laden with rice and divert it to their headquarters.

He paid an architect to design a house for him, and had it built far enough under the estimate (not too difficult a feat in those years of falling prices) to be able to afford a swimming pool.

He jumped as high in the air as he could and jumped backwards over the fence. She could see the gleeful expression on his face as he dared her to attempt the same feat.

affair, business

6.11 **Affair** is a very general word with several meanings. One meaning is an event or series of events which is thought about with disapproval because there might be an element of dishonesty or criminality.

They argued that the letter bombs and equipment in Mr Byrne's flat had been planted. Certainly, the affair seemed to have been conducted in an extremely amateurish way.

The theft of $10,000 was serious enough, or so the police thought. They found his assertion that he had also tried to assassinate the Vice-President scarcely credible. The full truth of the affair was hushed up until 1993.

Why would he take the dog along with him at the risk of being bitten? Odder still, why had the dog followed this stranger? Leonora sighed. None of the questions could be answered. Everything about this affair offended her innate sense of order.

Business too can mean a happening of some kind. It sometimes suggests a complicated or difficult activity, a puzzling event, or a problem.

A full medical history and examination will be carried out of both of you. The whole business may be rather depressing, and you could well be letting yourself in for a whole series of tests and investigations spanning several years.

Finishing his drink, he went to bed, a business easily accomplished by him these days as he simply took off some clothes and crawled under the sheets.

crisis, difficulty, problem, dilemma

6.12 An unfortunate situation, or at any rate one requiring a difficult decision, can be seen as a **crisis**, a **difficulty**, a **problem**, or a **dilemma**.

Nearly all the factories in the nation have closed, and food and money are scarce. News of this crisis is only beginning to spread beyond its borders.

Though the small body was cold and senseless, the doctor could detect a faint pulse and he was able to massage him back to consciousness. The child survived this crisis to make a complete recovery.

The industry is a remarkably secretive one and both sellers and buyers are reluctant to reveal the cost of transactions. To these difficulties should be added those of fluctuating sterling/dollar rates and significant and rapid changes in production costs.

Increased flexibility in the eyeball may cause vision to deteriorate as the day wears on. Another difficulty is that in about one in four patients, the effect of the operation is progressive, causing them to end up long-sighted.

Texts in exotic and unfamiliar foreign languages are far, far harder for singers to memorize than texts in their native languages. That has been a recurring problem with such operas.

Dilemma emphasizes the idea of a difficult choice, in which none of the alternative solutions is completely satisfactory.

I used to wonder what responsible choice we could make: using paper destroys trees while plastic pollutes the planet. Lately I've been avoiding this dilemma by bringing my own canvas bags when I go to the store.

The two aims might come into conflict: you will need to consider how you might steer your way through such a dilemma.

solution

6.13 Problems, whether described as such or not, need **solutions**.

'Rehabilitation is often thought of as restoring an area of land to its original conditions,' says the bank's report. 'However, this solution is rarely feasible. Often', it says, 'rehabilitation will mean simply restoring a cover of vegetation to eroding soils.'

accident, disaster, tragedy

6.14 An unfortunate event may be described as an **accident** (which could be serious or minor).

Three people died yesterday when a light aircraft crashed into trees and burst into flames soon after takeoff. The accident occurred at about 3 pm near Denton aerodrome.

You wouldn't be able to argue that your pregnancy was a little accident you couldn't prevent.

A really serious event or situation can be referred to as a **disaster** or a **tragedy**.

Thousands of persons were made homeless by the storm. The persons displaced by this disaster were advised to report to centers set up by the Red Cross and the Salvation Army.

Three months later Ian was dead. Luckily she had not been with him on the night he lost control of his car and careered into the woods. It was after that tragedy that Sharon decided to emigrate.

Although not a word about the tragedy appeared in the newspapers, the famine that raged in the 1930s throughout southern Russia was a matter of common knowledge.

On 30 July 1898 the most appalling tragedy struck. Thomas and his father were out in a boat when a sporting gun that was lying across Thomas's knees accidentally went off, killing his father.

incident

6.15 A difficult or unpleasant event, or perhaps simply an unusual one, can be referred to as an **incident**.

Ward started shouting and gesticulating and the broadcast was brought to an abrupt end. The incident made front page headlines.

If you have been the subject of a crime, try to find witnesses, and report the incident to the police.

In the second round of the 110 metres hurdles, Browne survived a fall, but dismissed the incident with a reassuring word.

There was just one outburst of firing during the night – a minor incident, compared to the pitched gun battle which took place yesterday.

Facts, statements, and ideas

6.16 You can refer back (or sometimes forwards) to a piece of text by classing the action or situation it describes as a definite fact or as something to be discussed (e.g. 'fact', 'topic') or perhaps as some kind of explanation for some other event or situation (e.g. 'purpose'). When the previous stretch of text describes 'verbal action', whether direct speech or not, you can refer to it using such nouns as 'answer', 'excuse', or 'suggestion'. If it is a 'thinking action', you can refer to it with a noun such as 'belief', 'idea', or 'theory'. Paragraphs **6.16–6.33** discuss nouns of this kind in more detail.

fact, factor

6.17 If you describe some event or situation as a **fact**, you accept it as undoubtedly true.

> *When they are told that they are suffering from some strange illness, they may not accept this straightaway. But gradually they will come to accept the fact.*
>
> *Something was convincing her that she was trapped, that escape was impossible. As this fact sank in, all her initial revulsion returned.*
>
> *We all had one thing in common, we had been selected to fight unwinnable parliamentary constituencies. Despite this fact we all learnt a great deal from our experiences.*

A **factor** is just one of the things or circumstances that could affect a situation.

> *Cameras can't make the kind of adjustments the brain does and this factor means that a drawing of a place and a photograph taken of the same spot look very different.*
>
> *It was a case of bad leadership, inefficient organization, lack of equipment, and various other factors.*

issue, matter, subject, topic

6.18 An **issue**, **matter**, **subject**, or **topic** can all refer to something that is thought about, discussed, or argued about. An 'issue' is often controversial.

> *Cider makers say they will be put out of business by Eurocrats who want to classify the drink as a wine because it is made from fruit. Duty on a pint could go up 500 per cent after the EC debates the issue this week.*

Andrew asked her again what she thought she had seen. She had been considering the matter. 'I did see him. I'm sure I did.'

He was tough on drug abuse. Sure, he'd been addicted himself but he had picked himself up and persevered with the cure. His unyielding attitude on this subject was that since he had done it, so could everyone.

I read extensively about the cholesterol issue and met most of the scientists conducting research on the topic.

The chapter refers only briefly to the suitability of different parrot species to conditions in captivity. A thorough discussion of this important topic is, to my mind, the most significant omission from this book.

She believes that cannabis is less harmful than alcohol and tobacco, both of which are legal. The women intend to raise the issue at their national conference. 'We have studied this subject very closely,' she says.

aspect, respect

6.19 An **aspect** can be a particular feature of a plan, problem, situation or activity.

In some ways I think avoiding the way back to smoking is more difficult than the stopping. Here are some helpful tips on this aspect of the problem.

'But who might want Mrs Brown dead? That's the next question for you to tackle.'—'We've already started on that aspect, sir.'

Respect can have a similar meaning. As a reference-back word it is often used in the phrases 'in this respect' and 'in that respect'.

He was determinedly cheerful, and seemed dedicated only to enjoying himself. In that respect he was like his mother. But Tony knew that behind his half-closed eyes Richard hid a much more complex nature.

Our superiors were every bit as tied to their jobs as we were. It was long hours for everybody. We may have been their inferiors in the job hierarchy, but at least in this respect we were their equals.

purpose, end, reason

6.20 If you talk about a **purpose**, an **end**, or a **reason**, you are trying to explain some 'fact', or, for example, why something may happen. 'For this purpose' and 'to this end' both refer back to some plan or intention, and then describe whatever is done to achieve the purpose.

'For this reason' points back to the reason why something, about to be explained, happened or will happen.

One poor soldier, whose leg they were about to amputate, having been laid upon a table for this purpose, had the other leg taken off by another cannon ball in the very middle of the operation.

When I go there it may be necessary for me to purchase the goodwill of certain influential men. For this purpose I have a fair amount of gold.

With archive film of the period now available, my first plan was to make an hour-long television documentary, and to this end I telephoned the BBC in London.

The world can, he believes, be designed so that behaviour likely to be punished seldom or never occurs: to this end, control of the population as a whole must be delegated to specialists, to police, priests, teachers, therapists and so on.

I'm interested to find out what's universally alike in human behaviour and for this reason I want to see cultures which have not yet had any contact with the outside world.

The job sometimes entailed physically searching for the victim, often under fire. It was for this reason that the people who flew the rescue helicopters were treated with considerable respect.

announcement, comment, declaration, message, remark, statement

6.21 Nouns for 'verbal actions' often refer directly to the actual words spoken or written.

His eyes gleaming, the man went on, 'The original tables have hidden drawers in them. It's said that one of them holds a great secret.' This announcement startled the three girls.

But I said briskly, 'Oh, I don't know. I should think most women would act like that in her position.' She looked slightly taken aback. I wondered if she resented my comment.

The Minister denied that he would resign. He made his declaration as he arrived for lunch at the headquarters of the Arts Council in London.

Attached was a small card and on it a single line in Arabic. Belle's knowledge of written Arabic was scant, and although she had examined the card she had not understood the message.

He read the telephone number, and the message. It was from Ben Gibson. He had tried to ring Arnold; would Arnold be kind enough to ring him back? (Note how 'message' here refers forwards.)

'I know she must be sad that Gran died, but money's always a great consolation.'—'Now, now, Roger, I'm sure you didn't mean it, but that remark was in very poor taste.'

'There was a team of policemen here all evening after dinner,' he said. To his surprise Milton accepted the statement without question.

account, description, information, reference

6.22 Other general nouns referring to some sort of writing or speaking include **account**, **description**, **information**, and **reference**.

The book tells us that the Archbishop of London, in union with the bishops and nobles of the land, made Arthur, then a youth of fifteen years of age, King of Britain in the year 516. Although no mention is here made of his coronation in London, it seems to be implied in this account.

'Well, Robert. So you're going to be one of our avenging angels.' Robert did not particularly relish the description.

'I think I was home by about quarter past four. I know I had afternoon tea as soon as I got in.'—'I see,' I said. My mind was chewing over this information.

Somebody described Barnett and his staff as a black hole surrounded by a vacuum. Quite good, yes. Although Williams laughed at this reference to the current chairman, his mind was elsewhere.

belief, conclusion, idea, plan, theory, view, viewpoint

6.23 Some nouns refer particularly to mental processes, though these processes may of course be expressed later in speech or writing.

If you have a particular **belief**, you feel sure that something is true.

In fact I thought she must be dead by now, though I had no reason for this belief since she was younger than I am.

Any form of racism is distressing to witness, but Suki found it even more disturbing to encounter such beliefs amongst her own community.

A **conclusion** is the result of thinking about something carefully.

He must have dropped his shoes when he sank in the canal. Just as he came to that conclusion the light from the windows disappeared.

'You mean somebody tried to kill us?' Bess asked. Nancy frowned. 'I don't think we can draw that conclusion from the evidence,' she said slowly.

An **idea** is sometimes similar to a 'belief', an 'opinion', or a 'theory'; at other times, its meaning is closer to a 'suggestion' or a 'piece of advice'.

He doesn't know I'm here because the idea hasn't occurred to him.

What better place to start the TV series than the island of Corfu where I had lived as a child. I was pleased with this idea since I had not visited the island for many years.

We were a player short and the priority was to determine whether Geoff Cook would be joining us. Frankly, I believed he would, as he had earlier seemed quite keen on the idea.

A **plan** is a way of doing something that you decide on beforehand.

The French President and the German Chancellor have proposed a joint army corps that could be a basis for a European defence force. This plan was outlined in a letter to the leadership of the European Union.

She denied reports that the United States was to build a military training base in northern Peru. She said there were no such plans at present.

A **theory** is something that you believe is true although you cannot prove it.

I'll bet you this is where it happened, because these are the sort of scratches a woman's heels would make on the floor. To test my theory, I walked a few steps away and scraped my own high heel against the tile.

They were all overjoyed, and secretly, although I have no evidence to support the theory, I believe Her Royal Highness was equally pleased.

Both **view** and **viewpoint** mean roughly the same as 'opinion'.

I really believe that one is a doctor in order to save life, anywhere and at any time. For forty years I have never departed from this view.

As far as Galton was concerned, a person's intelligence was a relatively fixed quantity. This viewpoint of Galton's found a ready audience among American psychologists.

suggestion

6.24 A **suggestion** is basically an idea or a plan that you offer (in speaking or writing) to someone else. Sometimes, therefore, it means much the same as an 'idea', or perhaps a 'theory' that would explain something.

People in the town started saying we were burning bodies. But it is not true. Until then, no one had even made such a suggestion.

A rumour went round the capital that he had heart disease. Officials would not comment on this suggestion, even to deny it.

At other times a 'suggestion' is an idea that could be acted upon.

Trade union leaders appealed for the government to suspend the price rise until Monday. But this suggestion was rejected by the finance minister.

'I shall speak to him myself,' Nina said firmly. 'If you wish, dear,' Tom sighed. He knew from experience that if he opposed the suggestion too violently Nina would become more obstinate.

promise, question, request, answer, reply, response

6.25 Several nouns often refer to particular types of actual speech (though they can also refer to written language.) These nouns include **promise**, **question**, **request**, **answer**, and **reply**.

'Paloma,' she whispered, 'Paloma, I'm here. I've come to take you home.' She made the promise for both of them.

He kept Paul talking, asking questions about the hotel. 'Did the Kemptons own it? Or merely manage it? Was it they who had extended it?' And among such questions he slipped in more personal ones.

'Now, please leave me alone.' He ignored her request. 'So I have done something to upset you?. What?'

'There must have been dozens of people who'd seen him.' Connors had a ready answer. 'He was obviously wearing a wig. Nobody would connect the man in your photo with him.'

'I presume you kissed her, did you?'—'Yes.' The reply was almost a whisper.

Response sometimes roughly means an 'answer' or 'reply', but it is less neutral because it suggests an emotional or psychological reaction of some sort. (It can also means a reaction that is not expressed in words at all.)

The report brought this response from one local inhabitant: 'Your broadcast today has left me a bit confused'.

Laura then relayed to her husband the psychoanalyst's shattering pronouncement. His response was delivered in a sharp tone of voice. 'How much did it cost you?!'

argument, assertion, claim, criticism, objection, opinion, point

6.26 People's attitudes, often strongly held and expressed, may be referred to in various ways. Both an **assertion** and a **claim** are firmly made statements.

'You take what you can get in this world, Johnny.' Pilarski held up his hand. 'No. You take what you deserve. No more, no less.' Charlie turned to me. 'We have this argument all the time.'

More political leaders tend to be assassinated in times, if not of peace, then at least when their countries are not fighting for survival in a formal state of war. Some evidence for that assertion will be discovered in the assassination index which forms part of this study.

I asked a woman in the factory how they coped with the terrible smell on bad days. 'Ach, we don't really notice it,' she said, with a wry smile that cancelled out the claim.

The claim is that such trees are alien and basically unattractive. This criticism needs, however, to be set against the fact that they account for less than a third of all woodland.

The result is a pattern of land use which represents only the preference of bureaucrats responding to the demands of pressure groups or vested interests. A further criticism of planning made by Hayek stresses the connection between economic and political freedom. ('A further criticism' shows that what came before was also criticism.)

The drinks trolley came along the aisle. Jeanne said it was too early for alcohol. But Ryle overrode her objection.

'I tell you, man, the whole thing is crazy!'—'Is that the opinion of the Press?'

'Is it something very valuable, then?' Alistair asked. 'Oh, no, it isn't valuable,' Henry answered, as if the point were not of much interest. (i.e. the point of whether it was valuable or not.)

accusation, allegation, threat

6.27 These are nouns which can refer to rather hostile or unfriendly remarks (which could of course also be expressed in writing).

He claimed I was jealous of Elliott. Which was a manifestly baseless accusation.

I am to be accused of treason and conspiracy. I not only admit the factual truth of the accusation. I regard that treason and that conspiracy as evidence of my patriotism.

It has often been alleged that Diana Winters practises witchcraft, and now she regretfully admits that the allegation can no longer be denied.

He accused the team of not working hard enough, and attacked the manager too, who was astonished by the allegation.

'I see your arm has not recovered yet. How would you like the other one broken?' Although the threat was suavely spoken, Kemp felt a spasm of fear.

advice, warning

6.28 A number of nouns refer to ways of telling people what they should or perhaps should not do. A **warning** advises people of something unpleasant that is likely to happen (particularly if they do not take some suggested action).

Arthritis patients, it is claimed, should not eat meat in any form. Many people who have followed this advice and eaten fresh vegetables and fruit have found a marked improvement in their health.

If you want my advice – which you've never taken in the past – keep out of the whole thing.

Gough and his staff had many times in the weeks prior to the attack alerted GHQ about the danger on the 5th Army front, but these warnings were ignored.

'There is the possibility not only of open murder but also of poison secretly administered: a most reliable source tells me that you should take very great care.'—'Thanks for the warning.'

apology, admission, confession, excuse, explanation, denial, refusal

6.29 An **apology** means saying sorry for something which you have done. If your offence or failure is serious, you might well make an **admission** or a **confession**.

'He'd certainly have reported anything irregular. I'm so sorry you've been inconvenienced.' Grudgingly the American accepted the apology.

'Yes, I'm sorry. It's my fault.' Latimer made the admission at once.

'Frankly I'd be ashamed if Yoller or my parents knew that we were friends.' This confession depressed Hunter even more.

Less apologetically, you might want to offer an **excuse** or an **explanation** for what you said or did.

'You said your dog didn't bite.'—'I'm sorry, but we thought you

wouldn't come if we said how bad he was,' Mrs Williams replied. This excuse sounded familiar.

'My car had a flat tyre...' Mather seemed wholly uninterested in the explanation.

The girl's mother had three kids from an earlier marriage, and so did her father. Then they had two more together. So the total is eight children, but the father and mother each had five. Even after this explanation, it took the rest of us a few minutes to get the point.

More angrily or indignantly, you might wish to express a **denial** that you ever said or did something, or a **refusal** to do something.

'Why were you in my room?'—'I wasn't in your room.' His denial was flat. I didn't know whether to believe him.

The baron picked up his revolver and turned to Federico. 'Go up to your room. Now,' he ordered him. 'No,' Federico replied. This refusal made the baron wince.

attitude, doubt, fear, guess, hope, objection, wish

6.30 Some words that refer to pieces of text describe personal attitudes.

Leo's view is that if a thing is worth doing, it's worth doing as well as it can possibly be done, so he will work just as hard at his hobby as at his career. One of the advantages of this attitude is that at any time a hobby can be turned into a career.

Could it really be argued, they asked, that governments were instituted to secure man's right to the pursuit of happiness? Was it as axiomatic as Jefferson proposed that all men were created equal? Despite these doubts and objections on the evening of 4 July 1776 the text of the American Declaration of Independence was formally signed.

She was afraid the children would compare her unfavourably with their mother and dislike her. I sympathised with this fear, which did indeed represent an unpalatable reality.

Around 1500 BC, the Hindu priesthood decided that creation had occurred 2 billion years ago. The accuracy of this guess was unsurpassed until the 20th century.

Men and women through the ages have testified that inner peace can be found through God despite excruciating pain. Euthanasia is the despair which rejects this hope.

I kept hoping that if I didn't look at them they would quietly go away. When I had finished, I opened my eyes and discovered that, unfortunately, my wish had been granted. There was only one person left in the audience.

compliment

6.31 A **compliment** is a kind remark you make to someone to show your approval or admiration.

'She's pretty,' says Erica, 'You resemble her a lot.' I smile appreciatively, though I cannot take the compliment seriously.

'I love watching you,' he said. 'The way you move.' She smiled at this compliment the way she always did.

rumour

6.32 A **rumour** is a piece of information that people repeat to other people. It may be pleasant but often is not; it may or may not be true.

He drank too much, so the rumour went.

I was told that flu was about but I didn't take the rumour seriously until one or two of my visitors began to disappear.

stuff

6.33 The word **stuff** is sometimes used to refer to remarks or ideas in a rather disapproving way. This is an informal, mainly spoken usage.

She wondered, for the hundredth or thousandth time, how Paul could say and write the things he did. Did he really believe that stuff?

What an extraordinary story. Do you actually propose to print stuff like that?

Ghosts and demons? Don't tell me you still believe in all that stuff!

Text as text

word, phrase, sentence, paragraph

6.34 A number of nouns can refer to a piece of spoken or written language as text.

'And now if you'd just like to give me an account of your own whereabouts after you left the party.'—'Of course! You want my alibi.' Conder rolled the word round his tongue in a way that made the questioner feel faintly ridiculous. (i.e. the word 'alibi'.)

Polly hurried into the house, muttering to herself. 'Doctor. Ambulance. Blanket to keep him warm. Police.' The last word had come unbidden to her mind and hastily she rejected it. His fall had been an accident.

'He would certainly have told you to do what I ask.' These words deprived me of all power of resistance. 'Very well, I'll do it,' I said.

What is all this about 'a far seashore'? Why have I got this phrase in my head? My thoughts are getting all mixed up.

'Do you mean it's a badge or a trademark or something?'—'I don't know.'—'Well, don't be too late if you can help it.' There had been an urgency in that last sentence which would not have been there if she had expected everything to go smoothly.

Now, he thought, I must think very carefully what to do. This sentence occupied his mind for some time to the exclusion of all else.

The report was scathingly satirical and closed with this paragraph: 'The young ladies at the Tallis School deserve better from our police department than they are getting. If Mr Lane is indeed the mystery intruder, as the police claim he is, he should have been more carefully watched.'

quotation

6.35 A **quotation** is a phrase or sentence taken from a book, play, or other piece of text which is repeated in the exact words.

'"The past is a foreign country", isn't that what you once quoted to me?'—'There's another half to the quotation: "They do things differently there."'

passage

6.36 A **passage** in a book or speech or other text is a section that you are specially considering. It could be of any length, even a couple of sentences, but it often means something longer than a single paragraph or that word would be used instead.

He had not tried to disguise in his diaries what he knew would happen to the soldiers. They were being sent back, he said, 'to torture, slavery and death'. Why had he not cut out this passage?
(i.e. the section relating to the fate of the soldiers.)

In one of Wodehouse's stories, Bertie extols the genius of his butler, Jeeves, finishing with this passage: 'There are no limits to Jeeves' brain-power. He virtually lives on fish.'

Consider this passage: 'You need to train yourself to prepare impromptu speeches, speak with enthusiasm, and use eye contact. The more you speak, the more you'll be able to use parts of an old speech in a new one.'

dialogue

6.37 A **dialogue** is a conversation between two people.

During dinner, the mother kept calling attention to the fact that her daughter needed to lose weight. Now it should be obvious that the public setting was not an appropriate place for such a dialogue.

Soon a voice announced that we were to have the opportunity of tasting the Ethiopian national dish, wot. A military-looking Englishman in the seat in front of me summoned the stewardess. 'What is this food?' he demanded. 'Yes, wot is that food,' said the stewardess. 'What?' said the man. 'Wot,' nodded the stewardess. 'It's what?' said the man. 'Yes, it's wot,' said the stewardess. 'What?' said the man. 'Wot,' agreed the stewardess. 'What?' 'Wot.' The dialogue was unstoppable. (The words 'what' and 'wot' sound exactly the same, and the Englishman is confused.)

7 Links in conversation

7.1 All the conjunctions, connectors, and other linking words used in writing can be used in speech, although some of them are rarely heard except in the most formal spoken contexts. Some words which are frequently used in speech as well as in writing are indicated as such in Chapters 1 and 2.

Additionally, there are some words and phrases that have rather special uses in speech, or are almost exclusively spoken.

Some conversational ***discourse markers*** link together the 'sentences' of a single speaker (although we don't in fact speak as neatly in sentences as we write). But sometimes these markers are used by a different speaker who carries on the conversation.

Hesitation noises

7.2 Sometimes when you are speaking you make a sound simply because you have not finished speaking, but are thinking what to say next. These sounds (they are hardly words) are usually indicated in writing by **er**, **erm**, **uh**, and so on. There are also various words that serve the same purpose.

7.3 To indicate that you are listening, you can make the sound **mm**, or you can say **yes**, **yeah**, **right**, or **oh right**. These may mean you agree, but may merely mean that you have heard. Also, people sometimes say **yeah** when they want to introduce a different point themselves.

> A: *And erm it's just unfortunate for people who want to watch something else, isn't it?*
> B: *Mm well yeah but erm the people who can't manage to see the match obviously want to see it on TV.*

> A: *How do governments and councils find out about what is happening to the populations?*
> B: *Yeah but...*
> A: *And how do they plan for what people are doing?*
> B: *Yeah but you... they've already got this information on computer or in a file.*

> A: *No one dares do anything to me; besides I wear glasses.*
> B: *Oh right.*

A: *It's the national language.*
B: *Yes indeed. Yeah I wasn't quite sure what you were saying there for a minute, yeah.*
A: *Oh right.*
B: *Yeah.*
A: *Erm I mean er it is a very difficult issue.*

A: *I didn't go this Thursday.*
B: *Oh right.*
A: *...which is rather a nuisance*

Fluency fillers

7.4 We sometimes refer to hesitation noises and words used like them as ***fluency fillers***, because they make the speaker sound more fluent, and they fill what would otherwise be silence. In this way they have functional importance in conversation – speakers can indicate that they have not finished speaking, that it is still their 'turn'; other people can indicate that they are listening, and following what is being said.

Words and phrases that are used as fluency fillers of course have meanings, which can form useful links in the content of a conversation. But at the beginning of an utterance their role in keeping the conversation going may be as important as their actual meaning.

A number of verb expressions are used in speech, sometimes for emphasis, but also as fillers. Paragraphs **7.5–7.8** deal with these.

I mean, you know, you see

7.5 You can use **I mean**, **you know**, and **you see** to emphasize what you are saying, often by explaining it further. You can say 'I mean...' or 'what I mean is...' in order to emphasize that you are explaining, even correcting, what you have said earlier. If you say 'you know' or 'you see', you are suggesting that the other person understands, or you are trying to persuade them to agree with you.

> *'It's true,' Nancy said, beginning to feel better. 'I mean, I do complain when Ned's in training.'*
>
> *They've had proportional representation in other countries and, you know, you sort of don't get anywhere. I mean the political system in this country is good basically.*
>
> *And when I say the war was over, I don't mean May '45, I mean autumn '44, when the Resistance had stopped blowing trains up.*

Because of the money I was persuaded by certain people in the forces to volunteer for four years and get extra money which I did. I mean at that age you're quite vulnerable, you listen to older people.

What I mean is that we spend most of our time not living in the moment. We're either regretting the past or worrying about the future.

He was short of money but you know he was mean as well.

Well, there's a lot of argument about that, you see.

You see, you're making a sweeping generalisation.

I don't know that it's an election issue. I mean I'm not sure. You see I have very mixed feelings over this.

7.6 However these phrases sometimes hardly seem more than fluency fillers.

But I mean this man was you know, he was sort of picking on the afflicted more than anything.

I said I'll, you know, feed the animals and then just go up the road.

And, er, you know, I mean I'd like to defend all accents really. I think, er, we all grow up with our culture.

Well now the dealer, erm, you see he's in Stoke-on-Trent.

You see but and then, I think I ought to write back and enclose these.

Well I don't think... I mean you see the Welsh and the Scots are very... are fiercely proud of their nationalities.

I mean it raises sort of ethical problems really doesn't it you know.

I mean I'd like to because I mean I suppose you know it must be fun to see but I mean I wouldn't do it.

you mean, do you know what I mean, if you see what I mean

7.7 People sometimes say **you mean** as a question to check that they have understood something that has been said.

A: *And anyway what made you think I'd change my mind just because he asked me?*
B: *You mean your father?*

To check that another person understands what you have said, you can say **do you know what I mean?, do you see what I mean?, if you see what I mean**, and similar phrases, although sometimes these phrases too seem to be little more than fluency fillers.

A: *Yes, where's your scar?*
B: *Well, it's between my shoulder blades. And it's on the right side but nearest the spine. Do you know what I mean? Right next to my spine.*

A: *I don't see anything wrong with her.*
B: *Oh it's sort of messy.*
A: *Well yeah.*
B: *Rather than... ha, ha...anything normal.*
A: *Yeah.*
B: *Know what I mean?*

Now that may be not good enough for you or me but it may be good enough for him. He may be doing the best job as he sees it. Do you see what I mean?

Will you ask her? But, you know, only if she really doesn't mind if you see what I mean.

A seminar is no better or worse than a conversation but we want both if you see what I mean.

I know, I see

7.8 If you say **I know**, you agree with an opinion that has been expressed or you accept the truth of what someone else has said.

A: *I mean they're not slums. They're nice houses, George.*
B: *I know, I know, I've seen them all being built.*

I see does not necessarily mean agreement, it simply means 'I understand what you are saying'.

A: *You line the cake tin and then sort of build the paper up round the outside.*
B: *Oh I see, yeah, I'm with you, yeah.*

Attracting attention, changing the topic

7.9 Various words and phrases are used to attract attention (in order to start a conversation) or to change the topic.

right, all right, okay

7.10 **Right**, **all right**, and **okay** (also written **OK**) are often used to change the topic. To some extent they mean 'yes, I've heard and I understand', but often with the implication that the speaker agree with what has been said so far. Possibly he or she thinks there i nothing more to say on this topic and so expects to move on to anothe topic – or perhaps to another action.

Right, that's it. I'm going to bed now.

'We have already suggested that on previous occasions.'—'All right, well we'll come back to that.'

Okay, so are we agreed on going north?

All right. So stand up on your left leg and get your right leg swinging round in a circular motion clockwise. All right that's what you've got to do. And then while you're doing that I want you to shake your head. Okay so you're standing on your left leg swinging your right leg clockwise. Difficult isn't it?

7.11 If the speaker is in a position of authority, then **all right** o **right** can have the force of a command.

The cop then rammed Kelly against the Land Rover, still on his knees. 'All right, hands behind you.'

7.12 If you say any of these words as a question, you are checkin whether the listener agrees or understands so far.

There's a little village a few miles north of Portsmouth, off the old London Road. Denmead. Ask for Stanmore Hall there. Or follow the signs, all right?

Anyway, don't tell me, let me guess. You're gonna show me a picture. A girl probably, right?

We had to cut a third of our staff. Terrible thing, letting people go, but that's business, right?

So you'll put down the number that you've calculated in percentage form. Right? You'll write three percent or minus two percent or minus twelve percent. Okay? On the top line.

Try to be more careful next time, okay?

7.13 If you say these words as a response, you may be saying that yo agree, but you may only be saying that you understand what has bee said. 'Oh right' is also possible here. (See also **7.3**.)

A: *I'll come with you, Doreen.*
B: *All right then.*

A: *It hasn't got a name yet.*
B: *Oh right.*

The following examples come from radio phone-in programmes. In each case, the radio presenter speaks first.

A: *We're getting towards the end of the programme and I want to squeeze another caller in, all right?*
B: *Right okay fine.*

A: *Dave, nice to talk to you.*
B: *All right.*
A: *Cheers mate, bye bye.*

A: *That is the commercial opposition down the road. You're talking to the the BBC.*
B: *Oh right, okay. Oh sorry okay right.*

now, well, so

7.14 Like 'right', 'all right', and 'okay', these three words – **now, well,** and **so** – can indicate that the speaker wants to change the topic or give some new piece of information. The different ways in which they do this are discussed in paragraphs **7.15–7.18**.

7.15 **Now** (and sometimes **now then**) can be used to attract attention and start a conversation.

'Now,' he said. 'We had better have another meeting, so that I can tell everyone.'

A: *Now then I want to ask you. Does angora involve cruelty to rabbits?*
B: *No, it's from an angora goat. It's nothing to do with rabbits.*

7.16 If you use **well** before changing the topic, you may be suggesting that you are going on to a new topic because everyone understands what has just been said. But sometimes it is little more than a filler.

He and I were special friends. He had taught me a few words of his language and I was able to make myself understood now and then. I taught him some of my words too. Well, Wamgum and I went out. The sun was high in the sky...

A: *I'm waiting for one of them to knock on my door.*
B: *Good man.*
A: *Because they're not going to get away very easily.*
B: *No. Well let us know what they say.*

A: *Go on then, carry on then. What do you want to talk about?*
B: *Well, I was just phoning up about er British Telecom really.*

A: *Can I have them delivered late afternoon?*
B: *Yeah.*
A: *No later than six, if that's possible.*
B: *No later than six. Well, we wouldn't do it later than six anyway.*

A: *By then it'll be too late.*
B: *Well, anyhow, we'll work that one out when the time comes.*

'Happy birthday, Leigh,' he said, leaning down to kiss me. I turned my cheek, but he kissed me quickly on the lips. 'Well now,' he said standing. 'I have some things to do in the office.'

7.17 **So** also suggests that what has been said is understood, and therefore the next statement or question follows.

I somehow got the impression you were telling me something. So what was it? So who was it?

A: *We used to have an assistant editor who could help us with it – on Wednesdays. What's happened to her by the way?*
B: *I don't know.*
A: *So who's doing her job?*

7.18 **Well** is often used as a sort of polite way of softening a criticism or a correction.

'I ought to go out and get something else.'—'Well, what's the matter with these eggs?' Sam put an arm round her. 'You had certain other things on your mind too.'
'He never mentioned that he was resigning.'—'Well, I don't think he would have done under the circumstances.'

You can also say 'well' if you are going to correct yourself.

Tell him we'll be there in three days time. Well, three and a half.
'Weren't you engaged to her?'—'No, well, no, not exactly.'

7.19 Well, well! shows surprise, or a sort of pretended surprise.

To his delight a familiar, tall, languid figure lowered itself down the steps. 'Well, well! I'm glad you're alive.'

'Well, well, well,' I crowed. 'Fancy that! What have we here!'

so what?

7.20 So what? (meaning 'What therefore follows?') is used as a way of saying that something is unimportant, or does not affect the situation in any way. It can sometimes sound rather rude.

A: *Toby, we're not students any more, you know.*
B: *So what? Why are you so conventional, all of a sudden?*

They are no better than me. They are just people who have got money. So what?

oh well, well then

7.21 Oh well and **well then** sometimes suggest a meaning of 'in that case' or 'since that is the case'.

A: *I've got to go and get some stamps.*
B: *Oh have you? Oh well, you can pick me up some airmail envelopes while you're there.*

A: *The publishers want the text in by the second of March.*
B: *Well then we can do it.*

then again, there again

7.22 You can use **then again** or **there again** to signal that you are about to add some new idea or fact that is rather different from what you or someone else has been saying, so you can use them to introduce an opposing argument. Both expressions are used in writing, but are particularly heard in speech. The meaning is roughly the same as 'on the other hand'.

The frog pauses, stock still. Possibly it is thinking what to do next, but then again possibly it has no recollection of what it did last.

I suppose I should be ashamed, she thought. But then again, why?

You might get them to take action, but then again you might not.

I do believe that in a decade from now there will be a significant and growing number of employee-controlled companies in the UK. But there again, I have always been an optimist.

A: *It's very easy to get a child to sit in front of a television, it's far easier than getting it to read a book.*
B: *But I mean, there again, but television is also very educational.*

oh, oh dear

7.23 **Oh** is an exclamation. It may be said to attract attention or to express some emotion (e.g. surprise, annoyance, or pleasure), or sometimes simply as a fluency filler.

Oh Ned, Nancy cried to herself, why did you have to leave me?

A: *He didn't send me a Valentine card.*
B: *Oh. Oh how disappointing.*

A: *Okay, what made you move to Old Windsor?*
B: *Well we thought it was a better place.*
A: *Oh I see yes.*

Oh dear also expresses emotions such as annoyance, sympathy, or disappointment.

A: *And Michael's out and I'm lonely.*
B: *Oh dear.*
A: *I feel like I want to cry.*
B: *Oh dear oh dear.*
A: *Poor me.*
B: *Poor you.*

by the way, incidentally

7.24 If you want to change the subject, you can say **by the way** or **incidentally**. You can also use these phrases if you want to suggest that you are giving some extra information that is not very important.

He didn't tell me, by the way; I found out by accident.

'She doesn't like being told about that kind of thing.' He paused and then said rather awkwardly. 'By the way, I suppose you cannot tell me when we shall be back in Bucharest?'

Let me remind you by the way, on Tuesday of next week, don't forget, the show is coming live from the Assembly Rooms in Derby.

You're listening to John Taynton on BBC Midlands Radio. The lines are going mad here. By the way if you want to try and get through, please be patient; the team are answering calls as quickly as they can.

It's really good of you and I'm immensely grateful, but I think I ought to stay here. Incidentally, how are you yourself?

speaking of . . . , talking of . . .

7.25 You can use these phrases to change the subject, but the new topic must have some verbal connection with what another person, or perhaps you yourself, have just been talking about.

'I keep remembering what you said. Forget about the past. Think of the future.'—'That's right. Speaking of the future, I'm going to be in London tomorrow. I would like to take you to dinner.'

'September's my favourite month. Still warm and sunny enough to sit outside during the day, but cool in the evening, and when everyone's safely home you can draw the curtains and be cosy.'—'Talking of being safely home,' Guy said, 'shouldn't Angie be back by now?'

look, listen

7.26 You can say **look** or **listen** to draw attention to what you are going to say next because you think it is important.

Look, I'm sorry. I didn't mean it.

Look, girl, you and me gotta talk!

Listen, I'm acting under the orders of the District Attorney.

Listen, how about some coffee?

If you say **look here** you are probably angry.

Now look here, you're wrong.

By six o'clock I was exhausted and at 9 o'clock I told the producer, 'Look here I'm going to leave at 10.'

guess what!, as it happens

7.27 You can say **guess what!** to attract attention before you mention some surprising fact.

Guess what! I've been promoted to manager!

We checked the dead guy's fingerprints, like we always do. Guess what. He wasn't one of our men at all.

As it happens sometimes stresses that a fact may be surprising, but i can also suggest that something is not very important.

> *'When did he last see a baseball match?'—'As it happens, last Sunday.'*
>
> *Genetics didn't have a damn thing to do with it, although, as it happens, my father was also a cop in New York.*
>
> *The minister would not comment on the case yesterday when, as it happened, he was visiting a forensic science laboratory.*

anyway, anyhow

7.28 These two words are often used in speech, rather like 'well' (se **7.16**) to change the topic, possibly by returning to something sai earlier.

> *Anyway, let's have some food.*
>
> *Anyway, to answer your question properly, no, I don't hate Jeffries himself.*
>
> *Anyhow, so we became friends and everything, and we call each other on the phone all the time.*

Or you can use one of these words to get to the most important point o what you are saying.

> *And I was thinking well if they've put him through that what are they going to put me through. And I thought well why postpone things. Why not just walk out now. So anyway I walked out and I came back here.*

Compare **2.54**, **3.5**.

Emphasizing a point

believe me

7.29 You can say **believe me** in order to emphasize that what you ar saying is true or important.

> *Look, I know you're in a hurry, but believe me, in this kind of situation hurry gets you nowhere. Take it easy, play it cool.*
>
> *You're doing fine, believe me. Fine.*
>
> *I've tried it and it does work, believe me.*

the fact is . . . , the thing is . . .

7.30 If you want to emphasize the truth of what you are saying, you can say **the fact is . . .** or **the fact of the matter is . . .**

> *I didn't have a chance to defend myself. I was sent home. And the fact is, a lot of other young people who were there are going to draw their own conclusions from that.*
>
> *Well, people often complain that CDs are cheaper in the States but the fact is that, of course, everything is cheaper in America.*
>
> *The fact of the matter is you have to decide.*

If you want to suggest an explanation or offer an excuse you can say **the fact is . . .** or **the thing is . . .**

> *Well, look love I'm sorry, the fact is I'm going to Greece tomorrow.*
>
> *I suppose the thing is, people wear things more now to please themselves and for comfort than maybe they used to.*
>
> *I mean, the thing is, of course, we have a different relationship with horses than we do with cattle and sheep and pigs, don't we?*
>
> *The thing is now, English is not my mother tongue, but I really loathe it when people can't speak correct grammar.*

You can also say **the thing is . . .** to emphasize a question to be answered or a problem to be solved.

> *The thing is, what do we do next?*
>
> *But the thing is, how am I going to know what standard I'm at?*

the point is . . .

7.31 You can use **the point is . . .** if you wish to emphasize the most important part of your argument.

> *And you see the point is, if you've got less staff, you've got more money to spend on books.*
>
> *I think there are differences, but the point is they were all looking for unskilled work 'cos they couldn't get skilled work.*
>
> *So many people today say 'Well that part of the Bible does not apply today'. But the point is, every part of the Bible applies today as regards principles.*

as I say, as I said, as you say

7.32 People sometimes emphasize a point by repeating it, and you can signal this with **as I say** or **as I said**. Perhaps a little surprisingly, these phrases do sometimes also appear in actual writing (not merely written representation of speech). However, the style in this case would be considered rather informal.

'So how would you rate him then? Mildly amusing or what?'— 'Amusing I suppose, but as I say he's not my type of comedian at all.'

Yeah, they were really lovely, the people in the group, but as I say it was a bit frustrating so I started hating it.

As I said most of the national rugby stadiums are all covered now, and all seater, and a lot of the top rugby clubs have got tremendous facilities now.

As I said at the beginning of this chapter, women have a lot of good business skills, although we tend to underrate ourselves.

You can also repeat or refer to someone else's earlier remark by using **as you say** – to show that you agree with it.

It is a very simple device, as you say, very much like a ballpoint pen.

'I understand your point of view completely,' he said. 'As you say, it could have happened to anyone.'

Informally, you can use 'like' instead of 'as', but this is considered incorrect by many people.

Like I say, I don't necessarily agree with everything he's done.

I think, like you say, the meetings are a good idea.

as far as

7.33 If you want to 'hedge' a remark, that is, you want to say you are not absolutely sure of your facts, but you think you are speaking the truth, you can use an expression such as **as far as I know**.

I was given no training whatever; nor was Peter, as far as I know.

Stan has always been a bachelor as far as I know, so my remarks about women were of no relevance to him.

As far as we know, no one has ever been killed by computer hacking.

7.34 **As far as I can see** and **as far as I'm concerned** imply that you are speaking personally or giving your personal opinion.

Lots has been lost and nothing as far as I can see has been gained.

It's a particular pleasure as far as I'm concerned because it's the first time we've had anybody from the literature department coming to talk to us.

Ending a conversation

7.35 You can signal the end of a conversation in many ways. Two common words for this are 'well' and 'anyway'.

Well I must dash. Wish me luck.

Well I must get back. I left the potatoes on.

Well I must be off.

A: *As you say, everything seems to change so quickly, doesn't it? Anyway, nice to have met you.*
B: *Okay, thank you, bye bye.*

8 Sentence adjuncts

8.1 Connectors, discussed in Chapters 2 and 3, are mainly single adverbs or other adverbials. They show how the speaker or writer sees the connection between two things that he or she is saying. For example, is one thing the result of another, or a particular example of it, or does the connector signal perhaps a repetition using different words? In their various uses, connectors share some meanings with conjunctions (Chapter 2) but they have a more detached role in sentence structure, and may indeed serve to show a link between separate sentences.

Another group of adverbials, also with a rather detached role in sentence structure, are ***sentence adjuncts*** (sometimes called ***disjuncts***). Unlike connectors they do not link one sentence (or sometimes one clause) to another, and are not grammatically speaking linking words. However, they have the important function of showing the writer's or speaker's attitude to the text. They are therefore included here because by helping to make this attitude clear they are important devices in making meaning clearer, thus 'linking' writer to reader.

8.2 Note that terminology in this area is variable. The term ***sentence adverb***, sometimes used by other writers, is avoided in this book because it can refer to both sentence adjuncts (the subject of this chapter) and connectors, that is, to any adverbial that stands apart from the rest of its sentence. In some grammars, ***sentence adjuncts*** are called ***disjuncts***, and ***connectors*** are called ***conjuncts***.

There are various kinds of sentence adjunct:

- Those that explain the way you are saying something. Examples are 'frankly', 'to be honest', and 'generally speaking'. These will be grouped together under the heading 'How you are speaking' (**8.4–8.16**). The words and phrases in this group are sometimes called ***style disjuncts***. They are mainly informal, and are particularly used in speech, in reporting spoken language, or in dialogues in novels.

- Those that explain your attitude to the likelihood or truth of what you are saying (**8.17–8.43**). Examples are 'certainly', 'no doubt', 'of course', and 'perhaps'.

- Those that show your attitude to what you are reporting or describing (**8.44–8.70**). You use them to give your opinion or judgement of whether something is good or bad. Examples are 'annoyingly', 'luckily', and 'understandably'.

- Those that indicate or emphasize your attitude to someone whose actions you are reporting (**8.71–8.87**). You use them to give your opinion of their behaviour. Examples are 'bravely', 'correctly', and 'foolishly'.

The words and phrases in the last three categories are sometimes called ***content disjuncts***, because they show your opinion of the contents of your remarks.

8.3 Although sentence adjuncts can appear in many different places in a sentence, the characteristic position is at the very beginning of a sentence, or, in a clause, immediately after the conjunction.

Frankly, Thomas, this question of your loan is beginning to worry me.

Lynda can't spend more time at home because, frankly, the family need the second income.

No doubt many will regard these as harsh words, but regrettably they are true.

Fortunately, the weather that winter was reasonably mild.

Correctly, he had trusted her integrity.

Another very common position is between the subject and the verb.

Many people, to my mind, spoil it for themselves.

The situation, frankly, struck me as all but hopeless.

He went for X-rays which fortunately showed his leg was not fractured.

The officials reportedly became annoyed.

We actually think we need more policemen.

When the verb group consists of more than one verb, the sentence adjunct often follows the first auxiliary.

The contract for this will no doubt be widely advertised.

He had obviously been hiding.

Classes had evidently ended.

Her husband was mysteriously killed.

It is now definitely accepted.

However, when the sole verb is part of the verb 'be', the sentence adjunct often follows.

I was frankly astonished at the degree to which different singers can affect the interpretation of a song.

The balance of power in Europe is fortunately stable and likely to be permanent.

Other positions in the sentence are possible, including the very end. In this position, as elsewhere, the detached relationship of a sentence adjunct to its sentence may be indicated by a comma, although a comma is not always necessary.

We're getting a little tired of it, frankly.

See you at the next meeting, no doubt.

Anyway, that hadn't got far, fortunately.

That's a mistake perhaps.

The company said yesterday, no doubt correctly, that it had increased its share of the beer market.

Given that a position somewhere after an intransitive verb or after a verb plus direct object is typically the position for manner adverbs, this position tends to be avoided by those sentence adjuncts which can also function as manner adverbs. This particularly affects some '-ly' adverbs. The following three examples show manner adverbs – adverbs which stress how the action of the verb is performed.

You can talk frankly to me.

Please speak clearly.

Did I pronounce your name correctly?

But where there is no possibility of misunderstanding, this sort of position is possible for such adverbs even when functioning as sentence adjuncts.

That's a mistake, clearly. (i.e. obviously.)

He's made a terrible muddle, frankly. (i.e. to be frank with you.)

And of course, with sentence adjuncts that are not also manner adverbs, there is no problem with this position.

That's a mistake perhaps.

It's only a theory, admittedly.

He's lost his job unfortunately.

For more details on the position of '-ly' adverbs, see **8.71**.

How you are speaking

personally

8.4 If you say that **personally** you think or believe something, you are in a sense implying that this may be an opinion not shared by others, but at the same time, like many of these style words, it can have a rather emphatic effect.

I had read the book with interest, but personally I thought it was greatly inferior to Lawrence's other work.

But that's your choice. Personally, I think you and Chris would be better off, far better off, here in the States.

I personally think that your custom of burning dead bodies is much more hygienic than burying them, as we do.

Personally I blame it on television.

Personally I think a jolly good smack occasionally never did a child any harm.

in my opinion, in my view, to my mind, from my point of view

8.5 You can also use other, less common, phrases to stress that you are saying what you personally think.

'Surely you have other sources of information.'—'I do. And I want to count you among them. You are eminently qualified in my opinion.'

There are several books on the market at the moment, which give listed remedies for various women's ailments. In my opinion these are too confusing and worse than useless to the uninitiated.

Most of the negotiations between unions and management break down because of a lack of trust, so the Church, in my view, has a role to play in the real world.

In my view the cost of living is not the most important thing for the working man to consider.

I have never discovered anything better than sailing to cut yourself off from the world and all its worries. But many people, to my mind, spoil it for themselves by racing.

Unfortunately you know a lot of bad music, from my point of view, gets into the charts.

The girl who'd just been appointed there was, from my point of view, utterly hopeless, useless.

honestly, frankly

8.6 Sometimes you may want to state an opinion or fact, and you think that this might be disappointing or upsetting. By using words such as **honestly** or **frankly**, you can emphasize the truth or firmness of your statement in a fairly polite way, while acknowledging that it might not please the other person. Notice the variants on these two single adverbs.

I've got lovely ideas for the front of the house, but quite honestly I don't know if it's worth it.

My mum belongs to the local choral society and quite honestly I ignored her singing meetings and things.

There's been gossip here. Honestly, Joan, I'd rather not go into detail.

I don't honestly know.

In all honesty, aren't there already far too many pages of scientific research published every week, every month, every year for us to read and absorb?

I'm desperately trying to remember whether it worked. I can't in all honesty remember whether it did or not.

Mr Cameron, my husband hasn't been well. It's... Frankly, it's not something I can explain over the phone.

The situation, frankly, struck me as all but hopeless.

This woman came up to me at a party and started paying me clumsy compliments. Frankly, I thought she must be drunk.

After I lost some hair I felt I looked frankly distasteful. (Note the unusual word order here.)

To be frank, I found her fascinating.

I'm here on business of a kind which requires me to carry large sums of money. To be frank, I would be happier if I had a pistol.

You may use **to be honest** when you are admitting something that perhaps you would rather not admit.

To be honest, I faint at the sight of blood.

I don't know if we could ever get to a normal life there, to be honest.

Compare **really, truly: 8.26**.

briefly, realistically, seriously, quite simply

8.7 There are several other '-ly' adverbs which you can use to make it clear how you are speaking. Here are some examples.

Briefly, we found out which soldiers wanted to desert; then we informed them that we would organize it when opportunity offered.

I can save you the trouble of reading it. Briefly, no less than nine of our agents have passed information to the enemy.

So what's new about tuberculosis that has renewed interest in the disease? Briefly, HIV.

Realistically, with many patients, there is no way to help the underlying problem without first tackling the addiction.

Hypnotists tell us that they cannot make us do anything that we would not normally want to do. Realistically, however, we all have only limited power with which to resist suggestions from those in authority.

'Keeping old age at bay is one reason for playing again,' he said. 'More seriously, I thoroughly enjoy the game and was pleased the club asked me to help in whatever capacity I could.'

'Anyway, thank you for making me get the dresses. Seriously, do I look OK?'—'You look terrific, Anastasia.' (Here 'seriously' is in a question, so the meaning is 'tell me truthfully'.)

Most of them, quite simply, drank.

Do not expect any personal revelations from me. Quite simply, the woman was an enigma.

Quite simply, these are the finest novels on magic ever written.

literally

8.8 **Literally** is a rather strange adverb. It can be used to emphasize the truth of what you are saying, that you are using the words with their exact, basic meaning.

We have planted literally thousands of trees.

With a wave of her hand she was off, literally running up the path before Sven realized what had happened.

But often this word is used purely for emphasis, and the literal meaning of the words could not possibly be true.

Dead fish literally carpeted the banks of the river downstream. (i.e. The banks of the river were covered in dead fish.)

You're a brilliant barrister, everybody says so. But you're an incurable romantic, darling, your head literally in the clouds. (i.e. Your mind is far away on other things.)

And it seemed to Bunbury that his companion in crime was almost literally driving by the seat of his pants and arguing off the top of his head. ('By the seat of one's pants' means 'by instinct' and 'off the top of one's head means 'without really thinking'; both these phrases can only be metaphorical.)

to be fair, in all fairness

8.9 As well as saying you want to be honest or to be frank, you can also claim to be fair . This is often when you are producing an opposing point to some criticism you have made or implied. A variant is **in all fairness**.

> *Until I or some other MPs get the opportunity to raise this matter in parliament , we will not know the government's position, though, to be fair, I believe ministers can't really do much about it anyway.*
>
> *'I'm disappointed in the BBC for giving it so much coverage.'—'I don't think it's just the BBC to be fair. I mean I think we're being bludgeoned by it in the newspapers.'*
>
> *He just picked up the notebook and marched silently from the room, several pairs of eyes following him in astonishment. To be fair to Geoff, this was an isolated instance; he does not usually behave like that.*
>
> *Some road-building schemes may be good, some are clearly bad and some dubious for various reasons. There is much more to be said, in all fairness, on both sides of the issue.*

Note: the adverb 'fairly' is not used as a sentence adjunct.

to put it . . . , to say the least

8.10 Another way of indicating how you are speaking is to say that you are 'putting', that is expressing, your ideas in a particular way. Commonest of these expressions are **to put it mildly . . .**, **to put it bluntly . . .**, and **to put it crudely . . .**, but many variants are possible. Here are some examples.

> *In the circumstances he was being pretty brave, to put it mildly.* (i.e. He was being extremely brave.)
>
> *Regrettably, alongside the real figures, a small number of women whose historical standing is, to put it mildly, more than a little doubtful have been taken to the hearts of feminists.* (i.e. Some fairly unimportant historical women have been presented by feminists as important.)
>
> *They are family orientated holidays and to put it bluntly they don't want old people there. It's not a nice thing to say, but families don't want them.*
>
> *We cannot, to put it crudely, open a baby's head and look inside.*
>
> *'You still love her, I think.'—'Oh yes,' Villiers said. 'Loving is easy. It's the living together that's so damned hard.'—'So what was the problem?'—'To put it simply, my work.'*
>
> *Some management games, in which young stockbrokers hunted one another around country estates armed with toy guns, were, to put it charitably, eccentric.*

To say the least roughly means 'to put it mildly'; that is, you are being polite and could have expressed your opinion in much stronger terms.

The evidence for all these charges seems, to say the least, unlikely to prove convincing in court.

Conversation in the room during the meal was, to say the least, difficult.

8.11 Note: **to put it another way** is roughly equivalent to 'in other words'. So it is a rewording phrase. See **3.15**.

Why should you believe a word they say? Or, to put it another way, how can you decide which words to believe?

generally/broadly/roughly speaking, in general

8.12 Sometimes you actually use the word **speaking** to make it clear how you are speaking (or indeed writing).

Generally speaking, **broadly speaking**, and **roughly speaking** mean that what you are saying is roughly or usually the case.

Generally speaking, even very young children are quite good at making the most of their pocket-money.

The refugees who were to be involved in the resettlement programmes fell, broadly speaking, into two categories.

So we've established a norm that, roughly speaking pay goes up by three percent a year, okay?

In general has a similar meaning.

Human freedom in general means the free exercise of human ingenuity in the satisfaction of an ever-widening range of desires.

In general, they like quick results so anything requiring long periods of study or work is not likely to appeal.

In general, short-acting drugs are better for this condition than those with a prolonged action.

'Speaking' in other ways

8.13 **Strictly speaking** means that you are claiming to be very accurate and precise.

Somebody pointed out that, strictly speaking, electricity was a discovery, not an invention.

'Can I leave money to my cat?'—'Strictly speaking, an animal can't inherit, although an animal charity can.'

It does help to remember that they're referring to a single point. They're not referring to the whole structure strictly speaking.

8.14 You can also use phrases such as **technically speaking**, or **medically speaking**, which mean that you are speaking from a technical or medical point of view. Often, though, 'technically speaking' means much the same as 'strictly speaking'.

Savings are, technically speaking, that part of income which is set aside, to be translated later into spending or investment.

Sometimes the monasteries made too many demands on the peasants who worked on their lands, although technically speaking, each monk was supposed to go and beg for his food.

The crews are fit and, medically speaking, we have ensured that this fleet is one of the best equipped for trans-ocean racing.

Women, statistically speaking, receive 75 per cent of the average wage for men.

as it were, so to speak, in a manner of speaking

8.15 If you use the phrases **as it were** or **so to speak** you are saying that you are not using quite the right words. This may be because you cannot think of exactly the right words, although your statement is more or less true. Alternatively, you may be pointing out that you are speaking metaphorically or using an idiom. Both phrases are common in speech. **In a manner of speaking** is a less frequent variant.

Suddenly, overnight as it were, South Africa was part of not just the Olympics but the big wide world.

We don't start and invent, as it were, on a piece of paper, these new chemicals.

Health-care workers, police and others accept the saving of lives as an everyday occurrence – another day at the office, as it were.

Another of Alistair's brilliant ideas was to have me start the programme and set the scene while standing, as it were, hand in hand with a white rhino.

You can't even trust yourself so to speak, cos the habit, the addiction is stronger than you are.

I ought not to tell you but I will, since you're in the family, so to speak.

Were she not his best friend's niece, he would deal more sharply with her whining. Tell her where to get off, so to speak. (If you 'tell someone where to get off', you complain about their behaviour and tell them to stop it.)

Oh you know how it is when you work with people but don't mix with them socially. You know them and you don't, in a manner of speaking.

in retrospect, with hindsight, on reflection

8.16 Sometimes you may want to say you have changed your opinion about something now that you can look back on it. There are several expressions which you can use with the meaning of 'when I/you think about it'.

In retrospect our responsibility looks daunting, but at the time it did not worry us in the least.

It might be thought that my work would have suffered from my obsession, but in retrospect I can see that during that period I reached the zenith of my career.

As ever stubborn, I could not bring myself to agree with the board judgement, but with hindsight they were right. (i.e. I now realize they were right.)

The decision I then took was a faulty one. With hindsight, and a clear head, it would have been better to have surrendered.

Only my family and my self-belief got me through. On reflection, the year made me stronger. I sorted out my values.

He has just issued a statement saying that on reflection, he regretted the remarks and withdrew them.

Your opinion as to likelihood

8.17 The sentence adjuncts discussed in paragraphs **8.18–8.43** enable you to give your opinion as to how likely some event or state is.

of course

8.18 If you think that something is quite definitely true, and that your listener (or reader) could not possibly disagree (or you do not want to give them the chance to disagree!) you can use **of course** to emphasize the truth of what you are saying.

She's Paul's sister but of course, you know that.

Scotland Yard is of course called into these cases as a matter of routine.

Of course is also used in short, spoken answers to express agreement. Sometimes this can be very polite, but sometimes it can sound rather impatient ('That's so obvious, why say it?')

'Do you know Davina Norris?'—'Of course I do. Everybody knows Davina Norris.'

'But you wouldn't refuse?'—'Of course not'.

'Do you still need me?'—'But of course, my dear chap.'

'You never told me that.'— 'Of course I didn't.'

obviously, clearly, plainly, manifestly

8.19 These four adverbs could sometimes replace 'of course'. But they have a more 'external' meaning, a sense that your listener (or reader) must agree with you because the external situation or circumstances show that your statement is true, that what you are saying can be deduced from some objective facts. **Obviously** is the most frequently used of these three and the one most used in speech. **Manifestly** is fairly rare.

'But who's responsible, David?'—'Obviously somebody who wants the truth published as much as we want to publish it.'

A candidate must have capacity for technical understanding at a very advanced level and the ability to express himself clearly both orally and in writing. Enthusiasm and aptitude for the job is obviously essential.

I turned to my left to see a small boy with dark, inquisitive eyes staring up at me from the corner of the couch. He had obviously been hiding behind it.

You have suffered losses at some past date and obviously don't wish to do so again.

Obviously, at an eighty per cent tax rate there's going to be a lot more tax evasion.

One of the police officers took off his helmet. Clearly, he considered this was a method of defusing a dangerous situation.

She clutched something against her chest. It was a grey manilla envelope, and whatever it contained was clearly the cause of all this anxiety and tension.

Some of his good humour had now returned to him, but he was still plainly baffled and worried for his business.

The content of BBC news bulletins is manifestly dependent on the uncontrolled succession of events.

unmistakably

8.20 If something is **unmistakably** true, it is very obviously or clearly true. The facts could not possibly be otherwise.

Each was wearing a long white coat and one had a stethoscope round his neck. They were unmistakably doctors.

He kissed her warily. Instantly, unmistakably, he felt her recoil.

probably, perhaps, maybe, possibly

8.21 **Probably** means 'very likely'; **possibly** means 'not very likely'. **Perhaps** and **maybe** are somewhere in between these.

By the time he came to retire at least two of the young managers would probably be ready to take over.

Now she was ten, perhaps they would stop calling her 'little Bessie'.

The Americans had already helped him. Perhaps they might help him again.

Some soldiers have died, others have been wounded. Still others are missing and perhaps have drowned.

All sorts of stories seem to go around. Maybe people make them up because nothing is actually known.

They'll get him. Maybe not today, but sooner or later.

Artie went where he pleased, and saw whom he pleased. Possibly he liked the excitement of the risk.

likely

8.22 **Likely** by itself is an adjective in standard English, but with a qualifying word such as 'most', 'very', or 'quite' it is sometimes used as an adverb – though some people consider this incorrect. The meaning is similar to 'probably'.

I'll have to tell the police all about it and most likely they'll want to know why I came here.

The decisive event would most likely come in 1917.

During the day a sense had been growing in her that there was no point in going on expecting him because very likely he would never reappear.

These troops, he warned, would very likely encounter enemy cavalry.

No, quite likely, he would not have told me.

Quite likely, however, the refugees may resist making contact with charitable organizations.

potentially

8.23 If you say that something is **potentially** the case, you mean that it is not the case at present, but that it could become so, because the situation involved is capable of developing in this way. We often use the word when we fear that something could become dangerous or harmful in some way, but we can also use the word positively.

It would be impractical and potentially dangerous for anyone other than a local person, with total knowledge of the language and culture, to attempt to communicate with the kidnappers.

Here, potentially, is a machine that can learn from 'experience'.

Here is, potentially, a machine with something approaching a real brain.

Planners find themselves in a similar position, expected to offer decisions that will satisfy a number of people who are potentially or actually disputing the use of land.

actually, in (actual) fact, in point of fact

8.24 **Actually** is particularly used in spoken English. It emphasizes that you believe something is true, that something happened – particularly when you think that this will surprise your listeners. So you can use 'actually' when disagreeing with what someone else has said.

Well we actually ended up sitting in seats where the backs had been broken off.

We've asked for five but we actually think we need more. We think we need seven tape recorders.

He had a little dog called Ella which he brought with him and this dog actually used to go into battle with him and she was actually killed in a battle.

In fact (and the variants shown below) also emphasize that what you are saying is perhaps surprising. So again, it may contradict or contrast with what has just been said.

He waited what seemed an age, but was in fact one minute, for the whisky.

May I point out that 'grass snake' is a misnomer? A grass snake is in fact a large, legless lizard.

It hadn't damned well even snowed! In fact, rain was splattering the windows, which wasn't the same thing at all.

Well I mean what is happening to you is insanitary isn't it. It's a health hazard in actual fact.

Seafarers like me swear all the time, don't they? It's common language. In actual fact I've managed to conduct myself in here, I think, without using one swearword.

In actual fact you've only got fifteen days' water and it takes forty days to get rescued.

She met and eventually married a man considerably younger than herself who claimed to be a pilot with Air France. In point of fact he was a chauffeur working for a car-hire firm.

as a matter of fact

3.25 **As a matter of fact** is similar in meaning to the phrases above, and can emphasize the information that follows.

It's not just an old wives' tale, you know, that full moons and madness have an affinity. As a matter of fact, as recently as last year at the University of Pennsylvania, an extremely interesting study was done along those lines.

Now some people have such confidence in the unborn child's hearing ability that they sing and talk to him and he actually responds! As a matter of fact, the unborn child has a completely developed auditory structure about half-way through pregnancy.

Sometimes **as a matter of fact** is used before offering an explanation or an excuse, or before admitting something.

As a matter of fact, there's a complication in the present situation which has made us rather careful of what we say to her.

really, truly

3.26 As sentence adjuncts both **really** and **truly** add emphasis, though sometimes in spoken English they seem little more than fluency fillers. 'Really', in particular, is very common in speech.

Well I think that it's such an infringement of the sovereignty that we've fought for long and hard in this country over a great many hundreds of years really.

And really I ought to write to him and tell him that I'm sending someone to see him.

I don't really know what to say to you about this.

I'm really looking forward to Thursday and seeing you all again.

She did not truly know him; theirs had been a brief afternoon encounter more than twelve years before.

You can also use **truly** to emphasize that what you are saying is true

Darling I respect your opinions, truly I do.

I am sorry, Stella. I truly forgot.

Truly, love is blind.

Note: both 'really' and 'truly' are often used in the sense of 'very', ju to emphasize an adjective or adverb. So in the following thr examples they are not sentence adjuncts:

I'm going to be very honest with you, Joey, because this is really important to me.

You need to take this really seriously.

Their efforts were truly remarkable.

8.27 A second use of **really** is to stress that the real facts are differe from what may appear to be the case.

Try to find out why they're really here and what it is they really want.

What some of these students really want is a parent to take them in hand and tell them what to do.

in reality

8.28 **In reality** has the second meaning of 'really' discussed i paragraph **8.27**. You are explaining the facts, which are not wh people may think.

Many of them wrongly assume that the surviving partner will inherit whereas, in reality, he or she may receive nothing.

In the distance a fox began to cry, in reality calling for a mate, but sounding as if in agonized torment.

surely

8.29 You can use **surely** when you think something is obvious must be true, but you are trying to persuade someone else of the trut of what you are saying. The meaning is 'I can't believe you don't agree with me' or 'You do agree, don't you?'

> *We had been sentenced in our absence, without an opportunity to plead our defence, which under the laws of natural justice is surely wrong.*
>
> *The police have surely questioned him thoroughly.* (i.e. I cannot believe they have not questioned him thoroughly.)
>
> *Well what about the ironing, John. I mean that's only about an hour isn't it? There's not a lot of work in that surely for a young strapping fellow like you.*
>
> *Surely you don't think I went off in my swimming costume, murdered my husband and pushed him into the water, and then returned to change?*

8.30 You can also use **surely** when you feel certain that something has happened, is happening, or will happen.

> *Name a famous conductor, and almost surely he has encountered difficulties.*
>
> *Food and drink culture in Britain is surely changing, has surely changed over the last two decades.*
>
> *Long before nuclear ores are exhausted, better energy sources will surely be developed.*

Slowly but surely emphasizes that, although an action happens gradually, it is definite or certain.

> *The number of women alcoholics is slowly but surely catching up on their male counterparts.*

8.31 You can also use **surely** meaning 'Yes, definitely', 'Yes, of course' in response to a remark by someone else.

> *'Would you all join me tonight?' 'Surely,' said Mather, 'That would be very kind.'*

definitely, certainly

8.32 Both **definitely** and **certainly** are frequently used in speech. You use them to emphasize the undoubted truth of what you are saying ('I am certain that...', 'It is certain that...'). 'Definitely' has the stronger meaning. It is not used in initial position (unless in a short remark such as 'Definitely not!').

This procedure requires a doctor who is a skilled expert. It definitely should not be done by yourself or by a beauty specialist.

Zinc is now definitely accepted as being essential for the combatting of infections.

You must be prepared to cope with unusual situations, local inadequacies and unpredictable events as and when they occur. Our kind of travel is definitely not suitable for people who expect to be cossetted or pampered.

Contrary to what some people believe, massage is not difficult to learn, although it is certainly true that someone will get better at it through practice.

What can be wrong with clean air? Nothing. Everybody wants it. I certainly support it.

I certainly don't agree with the drugs scene.

8.33 **Certainly**, when it begins a sentence, sometimes has a sligh meaning of concession ('It is admittedly true that...').

He didn't look as if he'd had a day's illness in his life. Certainly his operation hadn't made him lose weight.

It was rumoured that the town's traffic system had already cost the sanity of ten motorists. Certainly, one had been found slumped over the wheel of his car, sobbing in a highly emotional manner.

8.34 As a short answer, **certainly** is roughly the same as 'of course'.

'Well, sir, perhaps we could begin by your telling me just what you were doing Sunday night and Monday morning.'—'Certainly,' said Chantrey.

undoubtedly, without (any) doubt, doubtless, no doubt

8.35 These four expressions, though they look so similar, do not al mean the same.

Undoubtedly and **without (any) doubt** are the strongest. They suggest complete certainty ('There is no doubt at all that...', 'It is quite certain that...').

People who gave comfort or help to the enemy in this war are liable to be tried for treason. Some will undoubtedly be hanged.

'Teaching from a blackboard is boring and undoubtedly turns people off,' he claimed.

Conflict there undoubtedly was, but it was very one-sided.

Although hostile, Ron thought, Sammy was undoubtedly lonely.

Those who sink to drug abuse are without doubt the weakest and least desirable of the population.

Stress is without doubt the single most significant factor in raising blood pressure.

Without any doubt there is need for further change in Europe.

)oubtless** and **no doubt** are less strong, roughly meaning 'probably' ›r 'presumably'.

I've more to tell you than you doubtless read in the paper.

The turtles were removed from our bath (doubtless to the relief of the maids who serviced our room) and placed in a suitable container.

People who are told that they are unattractive, will no doubt eventually see themselves as being unattractive.

No doubt love for their fellow man played its part, but there were sound economic reasons too.

Jote: this use of 'no doubt' as a sentence adjunct should be listinguished from apparently similar uses in which 'no doubt' is ollowed by a 'that'-clause or a preposition such as 'about'. Here the neaning of 'no doubt' is one of complete certainty.

There was no doubt Greenfield was infatuated.

He had no doubt that the enemy must be ruthlessly crushed.

He will go back to London; there is no doubt about that.

ınquestionably, undeniably

.36 These two sentence adjuncts, commoner in writing than in peech, both have a meaning of certainty, but the emphasis is on the dea that the statement is so obviously true that it cannot be questioned ›r cannot be denied.

The squabblings of the art historians cease to matter. These paintings are unquestionably some of Italy's finest.

Undeniably, political stability and human progress in the country depend on greater economic success.

ıpparently, presumably, evidently, seemingly

.37 You can use any of these words to qualify the truth of your tatement. You are saying that something seems to be the case, but you lo not guarantee it.

If you use **apparently** you are saying that you have been told that something is true, or that 'it appears' so. **Seemingly** has a similar meaning, but is much less frequent.

Apparently your father was warned, but never said a word.

He talked to some of the children, apparently.

He had been found by a friend, apparently dead of a heart attack.

Her parents had seemingly borne their troubles well.

Evidently is similar to 'apparently', but stresses that there is some evidence to support your statement, often the direct evidence of what you or another person saw.

Voters are evidently angry now that he broke that promise.

Classes had evidently ended for the day because the campus was virtually deserted.

He bet a lot of money. Evidently, he lost a lot.

If you say **presumably**, you are saying what you presume to be the case, that is, what seems a reasonable assumption from what facts or circumstances you know.

He stayed here a short while. Presumably he booked in like every other visitor.

The new edition came out last month. So presumably the library will have that.

allegedly, supposedly, reportedly

8.38 These three words are commoner in writing than in speech. Even more than the four above, they qualify your commitment to the truth of what you are mentioning. With **allegedly** and **supposedly** you are distancing yourself; this is something other people believe, but which you very much doubt.

Faith healers have allegedly produced miracles just through the laying on of hands.

He regards socialization as now largely the preserve of the state. It is allegedly accomplished by means of education, welfare agencies and the subsidized arts.

A woman could rub this material into her face and it would supposedly eradicate the lines on her face.

From time to time during the slow journey, announcements were made over the loudspeaker system, supposedly to tell passengers the name of the next stop, but the voice was distorted and the information given in what appeared to be an unknown language.

Reportedly is more neutral ('It is reported that...'), and you probably do believe the report.

Her childhood was reportedly stressful.

The officials reportedly became annoyed when they learnt that the article in the New England Journal of Medicine did not mention their plan.

theoretically, in theory, in practice

.39 **In theory** and its variant, **theoretically**, imply that some action or state is said to happen or exist, or should happen or exist. But by using these words, you imply that the reality, what actually happens **in practice**, is different.

Although theoretically the land was owned by the State, the nobles and the monasteries held large estates, and peasants also owned land.

In theory at least, musical skills seem to presuppose intelligence of the conventional kind. Yet it is possible to find musically gifted individuals who score very low indeed on standard intelligence tests.

Though in theory he knew that he risked being killed or kidnapped, in practice he took for granted the immunity of the foreigner.

Yes I do consider that the present arrangments are inadequate. Not in theory, maybe, but definitely in practice.

officially, ideally, superficially, nominally, hypothetically

.40 These five adverbs all suggest – a bit like 'theoretically' – that what is being said contrasts with the truth. **Officially** means 'according to some official source', which the speaker doubts.

The meeting would be handled by his assistant. He, officially, would be somewhere else.

I can recall a time when officially your position didn't exist.

And so to this day we officially maintain that your department is only a figment of the popular imagination.

Ideally means that, in an ideal world, what is being said would be the case.

Ideally two sketch books are necessary: a small one, which will go in a large pocket, and a bigger one which will enable quite a large drawing to be made.

Ideally, the school should have spacious, open buildings and be in open grounds.

Ideally, all wine should declare any additives used during the winemaking process and should also list any pesticides or other chemicals introduced to the vineyard.

Superficially means 'on the surface' or 'at first glance'.

Many of these killers are frequently glib and superficially charming, helpful, sweet and kind.

Although superficially these industries seemed to be under public regulation, they were thus in fact mostly privately regulated.

Nominally suggests that the name or official description of somethir is misleading or not very accurate.

It was nominally a non-political trip, but this did not unduly inhibit the President's campaigning style.

Although they are both nominally, and I believe genuinely, volunteers, they are both constantly asking for money.

Hypothetically suggests that something is possible in theory, but n very likely.

There is no evidence that he knew, though it remains hypothetically possible.

Within every EU state there are thousands of employers which could hypothetically offer employment to a British graduate. However, such employers will very probably have well established recruitment practices in their home countries.

admittedly, arguably, conceivably

8.41 These three adverbs are mainly used in writing. **Admitted** has a meaning of concession – the writer admits something that some ways weakens his or her statement.

It is only a theory, admittedly, but the pieces fit together, and in my opinion it's worth pursuing.

To have survived acute thirst, a near drowning, and almost freezing to death is a tribute to his courage. Admittedly he had little choice in the matter.

Arguably says that it is possible to argue for a particular point of vie ('one could argue that . . .'). The writer may well believe the argumer but does not actually say. So 'arguably' can be seen as weakening th statement. However, in a sense, it may sometimes strengthen th statement, by suggesting that it is the result of a reasoned argument, and not simply one person's opinion.

> *Though Yeats was arguably the greatest modern English language poet, Eliot was undoubtedly the most important and influential.*
>
> *This satellite had saved thousands of lives and was arguably the most useful and efficient result of America's space program.*

Conceivably merely says that it is possible to 'conceive' or have a particular opinion, but the writer is not committed to it.

> *When we first got the letter I wondered if Mollie could conceivably have written it to herself.* (i.e. Was it possible to imagine that she had written it to herself?)

basically, essentially, fundamentally

8.42 These three words emphasize that you are mentioning the most important (the most basic, the most essential) aspects of the situation. Possibly more complicated details could be added, but what you are saying is true in a general way. All three words are used in speech and writing: **basically** is the most frequent, and the one most frequently used in speech.

> *Basically that argument was simply that the country could not afford to go on expanding non-productive sectors such as social services.*
>
> *Basically, a stroke is the result of damage to part of the brain caused by an interruption to its blood supply.*
>
> *The diet consists basically of fresh meat, fish, fruit and vegetables, with water to drink.*
>
> *In other words all societies are essentially capitalist, and all people are businessmen.*
>
> *Essentially, given the potential of modern technology and large-scale producing organizations, there is no technological reason for hunger or inadequate shelter, medical care and the like.*
>
> *Fundamentally, they were both thinking like bureaucrats. People who spent their lives in bureaucracies were typically afraid of breaking rules.*

hopefully

8.43 You can use **hopefully** instead of saying 'I hope' (or 'we hope') that something will happen. Some people think that this usage is incorrect, but it is widely used.

Angel and I were off to another life, another world, which was hopefully a much happier one than the one we had known at the orphanage.

Data for the scientific discoveries that made nuclear power possible has been collected by Nick Kollerstrom and will hopefully be published.

Hopefully some basic investigations will have already been carried out by the family doctor.

Your opinion or judgement of events

8.44 Sometimes when you report an event or describe something, yo do not just report it objectively, but you make clear your attitude to i your evaluation of whether it was good or bad, reasonable, surprisin or whatever. There are many sentence adjuncts which you can use t show your attitude – or sometimes the attitude of the people involve in the events you are reporting. Many of them are equivalent to a introductory clause: for example, 'surprisingly' is equivalent to 'It i surprising that...'

Sentence adjuncts suggesting that something was surprising (o expected and therefore not surprising) are covered in paragraph **8.45–8.57**. Opinions as to good and bad fortune are dealt with i paragraphs **8.58–8.62**. The following paragraphs (**8.63–8.70**) deal wit various other judgements, including the opinion that something wa important (**8.63**).

Something is surprising

surprisingly, remarkably, amazingly, astonishingly

8.45 Several words can indicate your surprise at what has happened of which 'surprisingly' is itself the most common.

The management has discovered unexpected benefits from employing over-50s. Surprisingly, they take fewer days off sick.

Her eyes met Nick's and she caught his happiness. Suddenly, surprisingly, she felt like a young girl again.

On this occasion, however, Rawlinson persevered, and Herbert surprisingly relented.

The factory had, remarkably, escaped Allied bombing.

Remarkably, the book contains not a single photograph.

I repeated the command once more and amazingly he obeyed me.

We thought the house had been empty for ten years. Amazingly, there was a telephone standing on the floor by the big windows.

In 1952, she had been the success story of the Hollywood year, the London–Broadway actress who had caught the critics' attention, and amazingly, the public's also.

Astonishingly, seven out of ten people in Britain have not made a will.

:uriously, strangely, oddly, interestingly, funnily

:.46 Sometimes you may want to emphasize that something was not ›nly surprising, but rather strange. **Interestingly** emphasizes that ›ou think your information is interesting, sometimes because it is :ontrary to what people might think.

He had a short beard which, curiously, served to make him look younger than his years.

Strangely, the idea that she might have left Berlin did not occur to me until I got to the station.

Around his neck, oddly, was a small green scarf.

Interestingly, it appears that those who are good at analytical, rational thinking, do not do so well when confronted with new circumstances.

'unnily must be followed by the adverb **enough**. The expression is nainly used in speech. All the other words discussed in this paragraph ıre also frequently followed by 'enough'.

The main ingredient is sugar, funnily enough.

I smiled and kissed him. Funnily enough, I was suddenly very hungry.

One of my guides in the desert with me got forty-three stings and was very ill. Curiously enough, I alone was not stung.

Strangely enough, the Hollywood gossip columnists and paparazzi showed similar respect and left the movie star couple pretty much alone.

The talk, oddly enough, was drifting towards politics.

Oddly enough, he performed well at school.

Interestingly enough, I found that there were more women working in Hollywood prior to 1920 than at any other time since.

mysteriously, inexplicably

8.47 If you say that something **mysteriously** happened, you are emphasizing that it was not just odd but that the thing was puzzling and is perhaps still an unsolved mystery.

> *A few months after the divorce, her husband was mysteriously killed by a hit-and-run driver. But he, the husband that is, hadn't changed his will yet, so she got all the money.*
>
> *Two psychiatrists from the famed Massachusetts General Hospital recently reported on a group of children who were mysteriously taken ill.*

Inexplicably means there was or is no explanation for what occurred.

> *Suddenly and inexplicably I began to sob. I hadn't cried for years and why now?*
>
> *The car pulled cautiously onto the grass and for a few moments it just sat there, inexplicably, with its engine running and its lights on.*

incredibly, unbelievably

8.48 If you use **incredibly** or **unbelievably**, you are saying that the statement is so extremely surprising that it is hard to believe, although it is true.

> *Incredibly, our army was not attacking, fearful that a hostile advance might mean death for the hostages.*
>
> *Incredibly, it seems that he was unaware that he had shaken off his pursuers.*
>
> *Unbelievably, the fourth game was also drawn.*
>
> *As we always tell prospective patients: if you want me to help you, you must be prepared to help yourself. Unbelievably this quickly eliminates about 40 percent of those who contact us.*

unexpectedly

8.49 If something happened **unexpectedly**, of course it was a surprise, but you are emphasizing that the people involved at the time were surprised, because they were not expecting it to happen.

> *They had driven unexpectedly down a one-way street and got away with it.*
>
> *Unexpectedly, I've been offered a wonderful job.*

coincidentally

8.50 If two things surprisingly happen at the same time or are surprisingly related in some way, but by chance (and not because of any plan), then this is **coincidentally**.

> *Nora spent most of her considerable leisure hours with her two adopted sisters, Magda and Suki, who were both coincidentally also residing in Canton.*
>
> *The new housing minister was a former aristocrat, to whom one of the now crumbling palaces, coincidentally, once belonged.*

Something is expected or appropriate

8.51 Sometimes you want to say that what happened was not a surprise but the opposite, something that was or could have been expected.

not surprisingly, unsurprisingly

8.52 One way of commenting that something does not surprise you is to use **not surprisingly**. (The other 'surprise' adverbs in **8.45** are not negated like this). **Unsurprisingly** is a less frequent variant.

> *Not surprisingly, the bodyguards opposing them were sometimes brutal also, and being male, expressed masculine brutality.*
>
> *The bad news was that the van, not surprisingly, was in an appalling condition and needed another thirty-six hours in the garage.*
>
> *It's an alphabetically ordered file, starting with A and finishing unsurprisingly perhaps with Z or something.*
>
> *Unsurprisingly, there is little enthusiasm in the City, or in Whitehall, for such wholesale reform.*

inevitably, predictably

8.53 If you think something was or is 'bound to happen' or bound to be the case, you can use **inevitably**, which literally means that something could not or cannot be avoided.

> *Rose was mostly liked and respected as an employer, but inevitably she had her critics.*
>
> *A more elderly population combined with rising home ownership rates will inevitably result in more elderly owners.*

The less common **predictably** suggests that anyone could have guessed in advance that something would happen or be the case.

First reports from the various hospitals and emergency services indicated that excessive use of force by the police had been responsible for the protestors' deaths. Predictably, public reaction was mixed.

Predictably, the new rule prohibiting goalkeepers from handling passes kicked deliberately towards them has caused initial confusion among even the most experienced.

There was silence round the table. Predictably it was broken by Janet.

necessarily, not necessarily

8.54 If you say something is **necessarily** the case, you are saying that logically it must be so. It thus is similar in meaning to 'inevitably' (though 'inevitably' also carries the sense of an unavoidable result).

The acquisition of valuable and extensive property thus necessarily requires the establishment of civil government.

There will necessarily have to be some further instructions.

Lynch firmly believed that the repository of all important knowledge in a small town was, necessarily, the chief barman of the local pub.

The opposite of this is **not necessarily**, which implies that some outcome or result is not inevitable, though it may, of course, happen in any case.

Of course if they didn't see him it doesn't necessarily mean he wasn't there.

A small child does not necessarily love his brothers and sisters: often he obviously does not.

Conscious envy is not necessarily destructive.

8.55 Note: **unnecessarily** is quite different – a comment on some action that you consider a waste of time (unnecessary, in fact!).

Elsie's mother came over with the coffee, unnecessarily carrying the cup on a tray.

'His throat's been cut,' I said unnecessarily, just to say something.

typically, characteristically

8.56 If you think something usually happens in the way you are describing, or someone has acted in the way you expect, you can use **typically** or **characteristically**. 'Typically' is the commoner word and frequently used in speech.

He had pleaded to be allowed to go there but typically at once began to have doubts once permission had been given.

Such calculations are typically made by bureaucratic decision.

I begged him to see another doctor. Characteristically he was unwilling.

I discovered I had, characteristically, lost the notebook. (i.e. I am always losing things.)

naturally, not unnaturally, understandably

8.57 If you say something is **naturally** the case you mean it is what is to be expected in the circumstances. ('Naturally' is therefore sometimes roughly equivalent to 'of course').

Everybody thinks you ought to take a holiday in any case. Will you come? All expenses paid, naturally.

She ran screaming into the street, blood running down her face, and the neighbours naturally rang the police.

Do you like bodies? Dead bodies? Naturally, you do not.

Some sort of platform, naturally, was necessary for Irene Byrd to stand on when she made her speech.

Not unnaturally has a more limited use – meaning something like 'not surprisingly'.

Different muscles in the body have, not unnaturally, different roles to play.

Barker still had his arm in plaster so, not unnaturally, press photographers appeared from nowhere and took photographs of the Prince about to be flown by a one-armed pilot.

Not unnaturally, the primary concern of the French army was the expulsion of the invader from French soil.

If you use **understandably** you are probably excusing some action or behaviour, again on the grounds that it is natural in the circumstances.

Many touchingly spoke to me of their painful experiences, but understandably declined to be filmed or directly quoted.

The syllabuses of military academies were understandably dominated by the study of conventional war.

Something is fortunate or unfortunate

8.58 Sometimes you comment that it was a good thing or a bad thing that a particular event happened.

happily, fortunately, luckily

8.59 You can use any of these three adverbs to express your pleasure or approval of what happens. **Happily**, which suggests that the speaker is happy about the event, and **fortunately**, which sometimes suggests an element of luck, are commoner than **luckily**. If you wish to mention who was fortunate or lucky, you can add a 'for'-phrase.

Even if they found a house that was within Mark's limit he could not obtain a mortgage without a regular income. Happily his mother-in-law came to the rescue and lent them the money.

Such discord is, happily, absent in my present parish.

Brian passed me a rope and I managed to pull myself up onto a wet, sloping ledge. Fortunately, the rock was rough and my deck shoes held.

Eventually the plane hit a house, but fortunately there was no fire.

Eight out of ten of us suffer this miserable condition at some time in our lives. Fortunately for most of us, it's an isolated event.

Once when she slipped, her bicycle headlamp fell out of her pocket and skidded away down the track; luckily it wasn't broken.

He simply called the police and luckily there was a squad car nearby, so they were caught.

unfortunately, sadly, unhappily, unluckily

8.60 Perhaps the majority of people are pessimistic. At any rate, **unfortunately** seems to be used – often in spoken English – more than 'fortunately'! **Sadly**, **unhappily**, and **unluckily** are other possibilities here.

In the course of time his wife had unfortunately become an invalid.

Unfortunately, my car broke down and I was stuck here while it was being repaired.

Sadly, what should have been a very minor incident ended in disaster.

They do have an endless stream of traffic hurtling by which, sadly, drowns the beautiful music.

Sadly for company morale, and perhaps for its future ability to recruit the best graduates, shocked employees read about the sackings in the newspapers.

This was not, unhappily, the view of everyone in the game.

Unhappily, although the traitor had been seized, the chief enemy agent had escaped.

Unhappily for you, things didn't work out as you'd planned.

Some people unluckily achieve suicide when they only meant to attempt it.

Unluckily for him the fraud officers were watching this flight too.

thankfully, mercifully, miraculously

8.61 If you feel relief that something has happened, or perhaps that something very unpleasant has stopped, you can say **thankfully** or **mercifully**. If you think that something is both fortunate and surprising, you can use **miraculously**. Particularly with 'mercifully' and 'miraculously', there may be a suggestion that God or fate was responsible for the fortunate event.

Thankfully, the land has so far escaped being developed.

There are, thankfully, exceptions to this approach.

That morning the Atlantic, mercifully, was calm and almost windless.

Mercifully there is no snow on the ground. Walking should not be hard.

Violent incidents were mercifully uncommon.

Miraculously, ten survivors had crawled out of the terrible wreckage, hysterical, astonished to be alive.

He used his skill as a negotiator to set up a conciliation force that since July has miraculously managed to keep the peace.

alas, tragically, regrettably, disappointingly

8.62 There are other sentence adjuncts commenting on how sad or tragic or regrettable or disappointing some event or circumstance was or is. These are some.

No, I married, but alas it has been a failure.

Alas, there are no longer any battles worth fighting.

Tragically and unexpectedly he died six months later.

The army has always claimed that the rebels fired first, and it seems probable that the two sides tragically misunderstood each other's intentions.

Business success is regrettably not about fairness but about making a profit.

Human beings regrettably are not omnipotent.

Regrettably, these authors supply no systematic evidence to document their views.

Hughie, rather disappointingly, chose an obscure restaurant.

Something is important

significantly, importantly

8.63 If you wish to stress that some event or circumstance has an important effect on something else you can use **significantly** or **importantly**. 'Importantly' as a sentence adjunct frequently appears in the phrases **more importantly** or **most importantly**.

His death was more than just his own end. More significantly, it marked the end of Indian resistance throughout the Midwest and South.

He ended, significantly, not with recommendations, but 'intentions'.

He'd made his point. More importantly, he'd distracted them from making enquiries about his affairs.

Don't hide your ambitions. Most importantly, you should ask what your area of responsibility, if any, will be.

It will depend on the drug you have been on, how long you have taken it, and, very importantly, how long it takes your body to get back to normal.

Other reactions

8.64 You can use various other sentence adjuncts to indicate a particular reaction to what you are mentioning.

ironically, paradoxically

8.65 **Ironically** often stresses that some event or circumstance is unexpected for the people involved, and possibly not what was hoped for.

And ironically, the evidence suggests that, by feeding animals and ourselves with antibiotics the bacteria and viruses develop resistance, so new drugs have to be invented.

Ironically, those who report feeling safest are statistically at highest risk – men.

Paradoxically stresses that something is not only contrary to what was expected, but also perhaps extraordinary or unreasonable.

Paradoxically, what we take to be objective, the real world outside us, they conceived as a spiritual phenomenon, a psychic event.

Intelligence often means being self-critical while, paradoxically, having confidence in what you are doing.

appropriately, conveniently

8.66 You can use **appropriately** or **conveniently**, as their literal meanings suggest, to indicate that something was appropriate or convenient, either in a general way, or from the point of view of a particular person.

Appropriately perhaps, since the main character is a moderately famous film actress, the other characters have only supporting roles.

Both children, unable to articulate the rage that might more appropriately be directed towards the parent, now begin to direct it towards each other.

The machines are conveniently located at Post Offices, leading retail outlets and Banks and Building Societies.

You can also use **conveniently** to indicate that something was convenient for the person involved, but that you disapprove.

Conveniently, he had developed amnesia about that part of his life.

'She's insane,' he thought, conveniently absolving himself from blame.

amusingly, annoyingly, suspiciously

8.67 These words indicate that you are amused or annoyed at what happened, or you feel that someone's behaviour arouses suspicion.

Amusingly, she tells her story from the point of view of a middle-aged woman doctor.

Annoyingly, the suitcase was just too big to fit into the cheap wardrobe in the bedroom.

Suspiciously, the 'sickness' rate jumps sharply on Fridays and Mondays.

absurdly, ridiculously

8.68 You use these words when you wish to comment that what happened was absurd or ridiculous.

'You're wearing Robyn's perfume!' Absurdly, he made it an accusation.

The death of someone you had, absurdly of course, always assumed would be there for you can be devastating.

The anxious expression on the doctor's face made her, ridiculously, feel sorrier for him than for herself.

preferably

8.69 You use **preferably** to state that you would prefer one thing to happen rather than another, or that one thing would be better than another.

She can't spend the night in that cottage. Preferably, leave her with friends.

Grab a friend, preferably a fellow job-seeker, and run through several mock interviews. Keep switching roles. Practise, practise, practise.

famously, notoriously

8.70 If you believe that the event or action you are recounting is well known, you can use **famously**. But if this is something bad you can use **notoriously**. Often, of course, the person or thing involved is famous (or notorious) too as a result.

As Descartes famously concludes: 'I think, therefore I am.'

As the late great manager of Liverpool, Bill Shankly, famously remarked: 'Football is not a matter of life and death; it's more important than that.'

There he fought cases that ended racial discrimination in housing contracts. Most famously, in 1954 he persuaded the Supreme Court that segregation in the public schools was unconstitutional.

He's no detective. Also, he's notoriously been no friend of the police.

I do not wish to set up as ideal the mindless, unending competition that notoriously drives men into early graves.

Your opinion of the people involved

8.71 Sometimes in reporting an action or some other behaviour you express an opinion on what happened that also applies to the person or people responsible. Most adverbs used in this way are derived from adjectives that could also apply to the subject. Thus, when you say 'The employee has unreasonably refused...' you also mean 'The employee was unreasonable to refuse...'

Many of these adjuncts are ordinary manner adverbs when used after the verb– simply describing *how* the action of the verb is done. But a position before the verb and nearer the beginning of the sentence has two effects:

- the adverb refers to the whole sentence or clause.
- the adverb stresses your judgement of whoever does the action.

Compare, for instance, these two sentences:

I was eating sensibly.

And you very sensibly declined to listen to this rubbish.

Of course in both cases, the subject of the sentence, out there 'in the real world', was sensible. But in the first sentence, the stress is on the way that person was eating – eating in a sensible way, choosing sensible food. And it does *not* mean 'I was sensible to eat'. The second sentence, by contrast, means 'You were sensible to decline to listen to this improper and insulting stuff.'

Or take another pair of sentences:

The enemy fought bravely and well.

Mr Kim bravely stood up to authority.

The first sentence tells us how the enemy fought – bravely and well. It says nothing about the enemy's decision to fight, and therefore cannot be reworded as 'The enemy were brave (to decide) to fight.' (Maybe, even, they did not want to fight, but were brave once they started.) By contrast, the second sentence stresses Mr Kim's bravery in the entire action – he was brave to stand up to authority, his action itself was brave.

Notice how these adjuncts offering opinions on people (**8.72–8.87**) differ from those in **8.44–8.70**, which are primarily passing judgement on events. We cannot generally, for example, reword our opinion of events by taking an adjective related to the sentence adjunct and applying it to the subject.

✗ *She was surprising to feel like a young girl again.*
✗ *I was inexplicable to begin to sob.*
✗ *Human beings are regrettable not to be omnipotent.*

reasonably, unreasonably

8.72 You can use these words when you think that someone is (or is not) reasonable in acting in a a particular way.

The earlier results were in line with expectations, so we can reasonably assume that the machine was not malfunctioning during the previous experiments.

The trouble is that the conventional training and development of marketing executives, quite reasonably, has focused on the external environment of customers.

The employee has unreasonably refused an offer of reinstatement from the employer.

A waiter threw a plate of curry at one of the customers, who not unreasonably felt aggrieved.

rightly, wrongly, correctly, incorrectly, justly, unjustly

8.73 Sometimes you think that someone was right (or wrong) in acting in the way they did, or that what has been done was correct or just – or the reverse. These are the words that you can use to suggest this.

The Pope's visit to this country has been rightly seen as an important exercise in Christian unity. (i.e. People were right to see it this way.)

Breast milk is quite rightly said to be the most perfect food for babies.

It is very wrong if parents encourage young children to go out, demand what they want and threaten violence if their demands are not met. If adults behaved like this they would be arrested, and rightly so.

Who got the money? The million pounds Captain Blake was wrongly accused of stealing?

The reason for the sheer boredom, as you correctly say, is unemployment.

As Haig correctly perceived, the resignation would not be seen as a 'purely personal matter' but as an acceptance of blame.

A man who, for instance, is a taxi-driver can correctly be described as 'self-employed'. (i.e. People are correct to describe a taxi-driver as self-employed.)

Many lady golfers incorrectly straighten the right knee in the backswing.

In our obituary of Arnold Jameson yesterday we incorrectly gave his Christian name as Andrew in the headline and in the first two paragraphs.

No government can justly claim authority unless it is based on the will of the people.

Scotland is justly proud of its magnificent scenery and famous heritage.

The Report of the Study Group condemned the action and implied, quite unjustly, that Waite alone had been responsible.

If, however, you want to stress that you have no opinion whether something was right or wrong, but you are just saying what happened, you can use **rightly or wrongly**.

The retreat also taught him, rightly or wrongly, how unreliable were his allies.

Rightly or wrongly, they believe they have been persecuted.

Whether rightly or wrongly, they criticize me.

consistently

8.74 If someone behaves **consistently**, they always act in the same way or maintain the same opinions or attitudes.

The truth is I've consistently exploited you.

Both animal and human studies have consistently demonstrated the significant effect oat bran has on cholesterol levels.

The choice could be restricted to people who have consistently followed some vocation or profession.

kindly, sincerely, politely, generously

8.75 You may want to use these words to praise someone for being kind, sincere, polite, or generous.

He had kindly brought them back after their visit to the animal sanctuary.

He had kindly invited us to what he called a light lunch.

Anyone who sincerely doesn't want to be biographized can cover his tracks while he's still alive.

I drove home, through the fires, and in Edgware Road, a policeman stopped me, and politely explained that there was no through route from here to Victoria.

Politely, Martin addressed remarks to her, but she would not reply.

Generously, he gave part of the money to his spokesman and the rest to his bodyguards.

Members should generously share work materials.

The owner of the company generously promised to invest £100,000 over a period of three years.

They had generously voted an exceptionally large sum for his inauguration.

8.76 Note: contrast the use of 'kindly' here with its use in requests and orders, where it is often ironic, and the speaker is either angrily requesting something, or has the authority to issue a command.

Will you kindly authorize your officer to remove his security bodyguard in the passage outside the door.

Would you kindly describe to us your activities on Thursday afternoon and evening.

You will kindly not instruct me in elementary physics.

Kindly cable your reply to these questions soonest possible.

'Please' is much safer as a request word, and would soften the requests here, although the third sentence ('You will...not') would still sound very annoyed.

bitterly, angrily, fiercely, crossly, resentfully

8.77 If someone is bitter about something, they are extremely angry and disappointed, often because they believe something is unfair or that they are being badly treated. **Bitterly** is therefore a very strong word. The far less common **resentfully** is similar in meaning.

She took his cold hand and held it, bitterly thinking that she was completely useless.

Most scientists bitterly oppose the move to patent these fragments because their function in the body is not yet known.

It never occurred to me to try for university myself, something I bitterly regret not doing.

For the second day running Ryle returned to the hotel during siesta and disturbed the dozing concierge, who resentfully produced his room key.

If you think that someone was angry when they did something you can use **angrily** or **fiercely** to describe their action. But 'fiercely' does not always suggest 'fierce' in the sense of angry or aggressive (e.g. 'a fierce animal'); it often means 'intensely' or 'very actively'.

> *Angrily, Joe socked Starkey on the jaw to knock him out.*
>
> *He put a hand over hers, but she angrily shook it off.*
>
> *He fiercely denied reports that he has made a secret deal.*
>
> *Fiercely, she assured me that she hated small men.*
>
> *Fiercely, he brushed away the tears from his eyes; he must force himself to do something.*

f you say that someone spoke or otherwise behaved **crossly** you are robably criticizing them for being annoyed.

> *'Oh, stop it!' she said with a sigh of irritation and crossly tugged her skirt down over her leg.*
>
> *'Never mind all that,' Mum said, crossly lugging her shopping bags. 'We've got to get home.'*

eluctantly, willingly, unwillingly

.78 If someone **reluctantly** or **unwillingly** does something, they idn't really want to do it.

> *Reluctantly the night porter decided that he would have to disturb the sleeping guests.*
>
> *Reluctantly, but with no real choice, John Kempton made up his mind.*
>
> *He had reluctantly come to admit that life outside the great cities had its advantages.*
>
> *She hesitated, then unwillingly related the episode of the breadknife.*

Villingly, of course, is the opposite.

> *He had willingly joined the conspiracy.*
>
> *They willingly assume responsibility for the success or failure of a venture and are answerable for all aspects of it.*

almly, casually, patiently, impatiently

.79 You can describe someone as acting **calmly** if you consider that hey were showing considerable self-control in a difficult situation.

> *The oddest thing was that Norman Davies calmly refused to admit the existence of the problem.*

Calmly, looking into the policeman's eyes, he repeated his account of his ill-timed walk.

If you say they were acting **casually**, you think they were not ver concerned, or at any rate pretending not to be very concerned abo what they were doing.

Bellamy casually reached for the oysters.

The Friar casually kicked a dog out of his way.

Casually, Fred said to one of the colleagues in his room, 'Has anybody seen the Chief of Staff since he returned?'

'What would you give for it, madam?' Casually she muttered a price.

If you use **patiently**, you are suggesting that someone is prepared wait, or to take their time.

A splodge of fake 'blood' began to trickle down his cheek. The make-up girl patiently mopped it up.

Patiently, the interrogating officers piece together the puzzle.

Impatiently is of course used to suggest the opposite.

He put the phone down and was turning away, his brain already clicking into gear, when it rang again. Impatiently he turned and picked it up.

thoughtfully, intelligently, shrewdly

8.80 You use these adverbs to comment that someone's behavio showed intelligent, clever, or careful thinking.

The Prime Minister has thoughtfully kept the industry job and several minor jobs unfilled, ready to reward loyalists.

He put the list away, and then took it out and studied it again. Thoughtfully, he added another item.

She, intelligently, left at about 11.45. I stayed talking.

The England captain intelligently played the ball wide to Steve MacManaman, magnificent again on the wing.

Shrewdly, he offered to provide financial backing on condition he became an equal partner.

Kate shrewdly recognised the usefulness of the work grapevine and managed it to her advantage.

bravely, courageously

8.81 If you say that someone **bravely** did something, or you use th even stronger word **courageously**, you clearly admire them for showing courage.

> *Once, long before, a snake had got loose in our living room, and my father had bravely trapped it in a shopping bag.*
>
> *Even more bravely, she is preparing to have her thick plait of red hair shorn and dyed white.*
>
> *In spite of spinal injuries he courageously returned to the burning wreck to rescue the ship's logbook.*

desperately

8.82 If you use **desperately** when talking about someone's actions, you are suggesting that they are in an extreme situation and possibly willing to risk almost anything to change it, though they may be acting without much hope of succeeding.

> *Desperately, he tried to think clearly.*
>
> *Mahoney desperately climbed and climbed towards that tiny square of light way up at the top of the well.*

proudly

8.83 If you use **proudly** when referring to someone's action, you may or may not admire them for it, depending partly on whether you think their pride is justified.

> *We proudly brought our new car home.*
>
> *She proudly declined all his attempts to help her with money.*
>
> *Proudly, he shows off the array of weaving and knitting machines.*
>
> *He proudly told Sharpe that he had stolen the food.*

wisely, sensibly, cleverly, prudently

8.84 You might consider someone was wise, sensible, or clever in acting the way they did. These are the words which you can use. **Prudently** suggests that the person was careful and avoided risks.

> *The pilot wisely decided to return to base as quickly as possible before the aircraft began to blaze.*
>
> *Wisely preparing for any outcome, the good nuns were not taking sides in the conflict.*
>
> *His aircraft hurtled towards the crowd, which wisely scattered as he hit the fence.*

Sensibly, successive councils had tried to retain the atmosphere of the town and there had been very little development.

The townspeople sensibly stayed indoors and closed their shutters.

Rather cleverly, he had now parked his car near the bar, so we had a good view of it.

After the funeral I questioned her about her age and she cleverly replied 'that was a printing error.'

In the face of growing hostility, the Imperial envoy prudently decided to withdraw his official support.

The majority of the population was against the Communists but prudently avoided making a public stand.

innocently

8.85 If someone behaves **innocently**, they possibly do not realize the significance of what they are doing, or possibly they do know but want to appear as if they do not.

One was always, you know, innocently committing some awful offence.

Innocently, I said I'd take a look round.

unwisely, foolishly, stupidly, rashly

8.86 If you consider that someone did not act wisely or sensibly, there are several adverbs for expressing this sort of judgement. They tend to be used in writing more than in speech.

Many members of the public unwisely assume that scientists must be better informed than themselves.

Unwisely, the Tibetans subsided within the sheltering shield of their mountains and tried to keep the rest of the world at bay.

The girl who took his call foolishly lost her note of the conversation.

Adam remembered how the Persian-speaking boys at school had laughed when, foolishly, he had confided his pet name.

The blackmailer had stupidly left his name and address on the magazine, and I tracked him down.

Yesterday stupidly I tried to get from one side of London to the other side, right.

Rashly he had criticised Mao's policies in a letter to the Soviet Communist party.

I spent nearly forty years writing books and made quite a lot of money, but I rashly gave most of it away.

carelessly, lazily, cunningly, wilfully, arrogantly, dishonestly, childishly

8.87 These are among several adverbs that are used to express very specific criticism.

Clements carelessly let the car wind itself up above the 110 kilometres-an-hour speed limit.

Soon after his birth, however, the queen's serving-woman carelessly falls asleep and the child vanishes.

One of the cricketers – who caught practically nothing from the bat all the week – snatched a bird out of the air after it had carelessly flown into the school building.

Lazily, she thought that she should be changing for dinner, and dismissed the thought at once.

Sharpe had an impulse to move back into the shelter of the trees, but lazily stayed where he was.

The staff cunningly got round this by serving drinks by the fire at 7.45pm and not showing us to the table until 8.

He has wilfully disregarded the instructions we gave him.

They arrogantly maintained that they had a mandate to govern.

Berkowitz had dishonestly handled stolen property.

In those days it was childishly believed that if government went round every industry to ensure that its exports exceeded its imports then, hey presto, balance of payments problems would disappear. (i.e. People were childish to believe this.)

Exercises

Exercise 1 (Chapter 1)

In each of the following pieces of text, join two sentences together using the words indicated in brackets. Make any other changes that are necessary. The first one has been done for you.

0) The house was built of good stone. And it was kept in good order. The garden also was kept in good order. (both...and)

   The house was built of good stone. And both it and the garden were kept in good order.

1) The beer and sandwich made him feel better because he had been hungry. It also made him feel better because for a while he could pretend that this was just a normal day. (both...and)

   ....

2) There was, she realized now, more than one way of looking at a key. It opened a door. It kept it locked. (both...and)

   ....

3) He doesn't look like his uncle. He doesn't look like his aunt. (either...or)

   ....

4) No one would know what became of them. No one would care what became of them. (either...or)

   ....

5) Sometimes you got the order. Sometimes you didn't get the order. (either...or)

   ....

6) Her nails weren't long. They weren't painted either. (neither...nor)

   ....

7) She didn't weep. She didn't despair. But she planned. (neither...nor)

....

8) Anthony was not a skilled mechanic. Fred wasn't a skilled mechanic either. (neither...nor)

....

9) Now when he moved his head he felt the pain of the bruise. He also heard the crinkle of the papers concealed in his pillow-case. (not only... but also)

....

0) She paid him a top salary. And the job kept him moving and happy. (not only... but)

....

1) He would be made familiar from maps with the layout of Geneva. He would be made familiar from a large-scale model too. (not only... but also)

....

2) Presumably the river carried the body down. It follows that this is where the body entered the water. (if...then)

....

3) Maybe land was nearby. If so, they might be able to obtain fuel and take off again before the plane was swallowed up by the sea. (if...then)

....

4) Maybe this view is right, but that would mean that perhaps we have been applying the wrong tests to the animal kingdom. (if...then)

....

Exercise 2 (Chapter 2)

Replace each of the following pieces of text with a new sentence or sentences as similar as possible in meaning to the original, but usin the words given in brackets. Make any other changes that are needed. The first one has been done for you.

0) While I was reaching for the glove compartment she was getting out of the car. (meanwhile)
I was reaching for the glove compartment.
Meanwhile, she was getting out of the car.

1) It was unfortunate that he was tone deaf. Otherwise he might have made a fortune as a singer. (if)
....

2) Though Tibetan was to be taught during the three years of primary school, all secondary education was in Chinese by Chinese teachers. (however)
....

3) You won't get any fruit off these trees unless you prune them. (otherwise)
....

4) Elsie poured out tea and after they'd all drunk a cup, Aunt Mamie announced that she was going up to rest. (soon afterwards)
....

5) They were living at the house with another young couple with their babies and a shared nanny. Meanwhile the war drew close and bombs began to fall on Glasgow. (while)
....

6) I wanted to be seen from the outer office but not overheard, so I moved the chair back from the doorway. (so that)
....

7) I was prescribed this medicinal cream for my face. I used it for about two to three years, generously applying it every morning. As a result my skin is now quite thin on my face. (so that)

....

8) 'And you'll go to Tasmania for your trout fishing?'—'I suppose I shall, unless the police want me to stay here.' (provided that)

....

9) Whereas Ireland worked as a team with clever passing among the forwards, England relied on individual efforts. (by contrast)

....

10) Whereas unemployment seems to have contributed to increasing crime rates, this has not generally resulted in more people being sent to prison for longer periods of time. (however)

....

11) Much as he had enjoyed the lively company of his friends in Edinburgh, his work, he felt, demanded solitude. (all the same)

....

12) While some UN sources expressed hope that a deal would be struck, the Americans were less optimistic. (on the other hand)

....

13) Although they knew it was wrong to steal a car, most of those interviewed, all under 17, did not consider themselves criminals. (despite)

....

14) 'I can't do anything for several days,' he said. 'There's an important murder trial going on and I'm the main police witness. It won't matter a lot, though.' (still)

....

15) Then she made some sandwiches and coffee and put them on a

tray to take into the sitting-room for their supper. While she was doing it Patrick and Margaret talked quietly. (meanwhile)

....

16) We had our money stolen on the last day. Otherwise we had a wonderful time there. (except that)

....

Exercise 3 (Chapter 2)

Some words and phrases look similar but meaning and usage are not the same. From the following pairs, choose the best words to complete the sentences.

1) by contrast on the contrary

a) Tobacconists, booksellers, and stationers also reported falling activity. .... chemists, grocers, shoe shops and leather stores all said business was better last month than in January.

b) There was no anxiety on the flight deck, no shouts of warning: ...., the pilots commented to each other on the awesome beauty, the majesty and tranquillity of what they were seeing.

c) There had been no elections, no campaigning, no consulting the people. ...., helpless civilians had been shot, the radio station closed down and a puppet government installed.

2) though although

a) It seemed that the new government was the only topic the King would allow to be spoken of, ... at the same time he would say almost nothing about it himself.

b) The tour continues through some beautiful wine towns whose vineyards can be visited and wines tasted. In truth, ..., the opportunities for tasting are fairly infrequent in this part of the tour.

c) It was such a pleasant town, barely a city, even .... it was the capital.

:) for that matter no matter

a) We haven't been a real world power since the end of the war, ... what we've pretended.

b) For some unexplained reason, ... how hot it would get, Eric never seemed to perspire.

c) The cabin was unlocked. It didn't even have a lock ....

) in case in any case

a) She went on with her search, knocking on each door before entering the room .... the occupant was lying down, or perhaps asleep.

b) But perhaps you have a private number just .... something interesting which I could pass on emerges in any conversation or discussion I might have.

c) The pale furnishing colours they had enjoyed in their last house were not going to be practical here. .... they wanted something different.

) given (that) granted (that)

a) She has health problems. .... that's not her fault, but all the rest is.

b) .... theory consists of a set of ideas, those ideas must come from somewhere.

c) I don't see what I can do for you, ... you have, I repeat, no evidence.

) all the same at the same time

a) 'I don't suppose you've any facts to support that?' 'No hard evidence,' Brand admitted. 'I thought not. .... I'd like to hear your story for myself.'

b) The only person I could think of asking was my husband, and yet .... he was the one I was supposed to be running away from.

c) 'There's nothing to be done for him. He's dead. This is one time the kiss of life won't help, ' she said. '.................., you were splendid trying to save him like that.'

7) above all after all

a) Each sentence ought to be balanced, so that it sounds right if it is read aloud; it should end before a reader runs out of breath. .... it should say exactly what it means, in the simplest way.

b) He earned a reputation for sound, logical and .... honest performances in the House of Commons.

c) He was beginning to feel foolish about criticizing the police. ...., what did he know about questioning murder suspects

8) in the meantime meanwhile

a) The BBC are trying to get independent confirmation of this story; ...., please do not use this version.

b) One of his ventures was an overseas bank. His son Nigel directed it. .... another of his sons, Ernest, was sent to prison in Hong Kong for corruption.

c) We need a new system which takes into account the real educational needs of London's children. ...., the government should stick to the present arrangements.

Exercise 4 (Chapter 2)

Some conjunctions have more than one meaning. Find expressions which best explain the different meanings of the words underlined. Here are some suggestions to help you. The first pair have been done for you.

all the time when	although	although . . . greatly
because	earlier than	from the time when
in order that	in the way that	more or less the same as
provided that	rather than	the whole time that
whereas	with the result that	

0) <u>As</u> he drew closer, picking his way through the rocks, he could se that his son was excited.

00) He felt ashamed that he had not offered to serve in the Frenc army <u>as</u> many other settlers had done.
Meaning: 0) all the time when .... 00) in the way that ....

1) I haven't been back since I left before the war as a girl.

2) Water containing high levels of nitrates or nitrites should not be given to babies, since these minerals increase the risk of blood disorders.
Meaning: 1) .... 2) ....

3) In the centre of the lawn a figure stood motionless. It must have stood there as long as she had.

4) He didn't care what the flowers were, as long as they were yellow.
Meaning: 3) .... 4) ....

5) She held the telephone firmly against her ear so that no telltale sound could leak out.

6) The effects of time and blackcurrant juice have healed her throat, so that she can speak normally again now.
Meaning: 5) .... 6) ....

7) He looked young and earnest, much as he'd always done.

8) You will always be welcome when you get back but much as I should like to see you, I believe it is best for you to stay where you are.
Meaning: 7) .... 8) ....

9) They'll kill you sooner than let an outsider cause trouble.

10) The Bank is likely to lower interest rates sooner than expected.
Meaning: 9) .... 10)..................................

11) While chemical control of pests is not the only option, its use far outstrips other techniques.

12) Meat and bread prices will go up three times, while tea, butter, and cigarettes will cost double.
Meaning: 11) .... 12) ....

Exercise 5 (Chapter 2)

Complete the sentences using the following conjunctions once each.

as though	even though	for	in case
lest	on condition that	so	until
wherever	yet		

1) We had no worries about where to get off .... we were to be met by our uncle.

2) She wore black of course, and she looked enchanting. He guessed, correctly, that Veronica never looked anything but enchanting, ... black suited her best of all.

3) I got here too early. I left home in plenty of time .... I had trouble finding the place.

4) They were allowed to play anywhere in the park .... it had a special playground.

5) A six o'clock start got him to the airport with half an hour to spare .... he bought two newspapers.

6) He would have to avoid saying anything to Ginny .... he bring the same fate on her.

7) He slashed the air with his sword .... it was a whip.

8) Nancy followed them, keeping a safe distance, sticking close to the trees .... there were any.

9) I will decide what programme of work will be carried out. You will not take any action .... you have precise instructions from me. Is that clear?

10) I will live with you .... you never look inside my handbag without my permission.

Exercise 6 (Chapters 2 and 3)

In each of the following pieces of text, choose the best connector from the underlined alternatives.

1) She was a good judge of character and felt he spoke the truth. Besides/Instead/Nevertheless she didn't care for him.

2) The traffic was so heavy that the driver went slowly and was often forced to stop. Soon, furthermore/however/moreover we were on a faster road, and we picked up speed.

3) She had thought she would be grateful for their company on the drive back to Algiers, but for one thing / instead / likewise they were making her nervous.

4) You can now telephone our credit card hotline on 0121 414 6203. Accordingly/Alternatively/Equally complete the order form and return it to the address printed.

5) Tom's mother had been determined that he should not become a coal miner like his father and brothers. Accordingly / All in all / At the same time, she had sent him away to live with her sister, who was married to a shopkeeper in Hereford.

6) I believe my career has been well spent. At last / At least / At the same time that is my view.

7) As one grows older, so all the body processes slow down and food is less well utilized than it once was. Extra vitamins are in addition / instead / therefore needed to compensate for this.

8) The recent recession has destroyed a high proportion of vacation jobs. Hence/However/Nonetheless, we would expect student debt to be on a sharp rise at present.

9) I take my two dogs with me everywhere I go. Even so / For that matter / So my friends are pretty used to them by now.

10) That's why I've come here today, to tell your mother that her brother needs more money. Well, that's my excuse, also/anyway/indeed.

11) This was not a well-travelled road. Even so / For example / Moreover, it was an extremely dusty one.

12) Disappointingly, though, the symptoms continued; indeed/otherwise/similarly it is only in the last few weeks or so that I have been free of them.

13) It is appropriate at the end of this important period to reflect upon a major development of benefit to all aircraft, namely / likewise / or rather, navigational and automatic piloting equipment.

14) He pulled a small enamel box out of the pocket of his jacket and placed it on the table in front of him. Next / Then again / Thus he tore a blank page from his notebook and folded it in two.

15) We will ensure that anything you ask for is delivered directly to your hotel room. Likewise/Otherwise/Thereby, if you wish to visit the ballet or opera, this too will be arranged.

Exercise 7 (Chapter 4)

Join each of the following pairs of sentences together into one sentence in the way indicated, and underline the 'that'-clauses or 'wh'-clauses you have made. The first one has been done for you.

0) He saw something. He didn't like it.
He didn't like what he saw. ....

1) I'll do something or other, and it will be well thought out.
Whatever ....

2) It must be Pete's brother! This suddenly dawned on me.
It ....

3) What are we looking for? We don't know.
We ....

4) This man is your brother. We are certain of it.
We ....

5) Something or other was going on in the investigation; he felt he was closer to it than he had been before.
He ....

6) Improved breathing would bring better co-ordination. This was the vital factor.
The ....

7) Why should they wish to look like that appalling man? It's beyond me.
It's..

8) We have 28 professionals. You can't run away from that fact.
You ....

9) The document has been wrongly dated and ought to read 1932 instead of 1931. This is clear from the contents.
From ....

10) Someone said history repeats itself first as tragedy, then as farce. They were right.
Whoever ....

11) I am going to say something. Please listen carefully.
Please ....

12) Who does it belong to? That's something they are still arguing over.
They ....

13) Whose money is it? That doesn't matter!
It ....

14) How should we handle this? Let's talk about it.
Let's ....

Exercise 8 (Chapter 4)

Rewrite the following, using non-finite or verbless clauses in place of the underlined clauses. The first one has been done for you, and extra help has been given with numbers 11, 15, and 17.

0) When he looked at his watch, he saw that it was half past five.
Looking at his watch, he saw that it was half past five.

1) After he left the hotel early in the morning, he headed for the public library, and took up his usual position on the steps.

....

2) He grew impatient if he was told that something could not be done because it had not been done before.

....

3) He stared vacantly at the people who were milling around as if they were unaware of the commotion.

....

4) They said they were so busy they would need a week before they took action.

....

5) Even when she was asked a direct question she scarcely bothered to answer.

....

6) These schemes should be fairer to taxpayers, but they would still be expensive, especially if they were available to all.

....

7) He poured himself another drink; he was unwilling to lose the moment and the memory.

....

8) I've heard that Joe Wilson, though he is unwilling to part with any money during his life, will leave everything to her after his death.

....

9) Do you think that while he was still in motion his cycle was kicked from behind?

....

10) How do we choose? When we have chosen, how do we know that this is the best choice?

....

11) She didn't realize it, but she was moving along the road, and she was unaware of its crystal-hard covering of ice.

Without ....

12) Because she realized that she was blocking his path, she stepped cautiously to one side.

....

13) Although they were unhappy with the opinion polls, Republicans argued yesterday that they would receive a boost from their convention in August.

....

14) He finished the tea and laid the cup aside, because he wasn't expecting her to answer.

....

15) Mother had had a fainting fit when she heard the news.

.... on ....

16) The doctors have been marvellous in the way they have explained everything.

....

17) Joanna startled Enid: she gave her an utterly inappropriate hug.

.... by ....

18) His eyes were fixed on the lake: he made the sort of meaningless remarks that the occasion required.

....

Exercise 9 (Chapter 5)

Say what the underlined items substitute for or refer to. The first one has been done for you.

0) 'How do you know no one else saw her?'— 'Someone might have, sir, but if so, they haven't come forward yet.'
if someone else saw her ....

1) He wanted to extend a hand, touch the body lying there, but he could not nerve himself to do so.
....

2) Send them along, and if they arrive before I leave, well and good. If not, the responsibility will be mine and you'll have done your duty.
....

3) Few drivers left the highway here, although there was a grassy area which made this possible.
....

4) They're nightmares. Terrible, hideous, frightening nightmares. I don't feel joy. I feel pain. But the first ones weren't like that.
a) ones ....
b) like that ....

5) He was trying to decide whether to advise Robin to go to a London hospital or to a local hospital in Sussex. Finally he thought he would advise the latter. When I asked his reason for this he replied that he thought the Sussex hospital a good one and that it would be much more pleasant for me, visiting Robin, to be in the country and not too far from home.
a) the latter ....
b) this ....
c) one ....
d) it ....

6) 'Have you any valuables anywhere else in the house that need checking?'—'I don't think so. My wife and I gave our son a great many things when he married. It seemed to us that that was the sensible thing to do.'

a) so ....

b) that ....

7) He would sit at his desk staring at the telephone, aware every moment that nothing was happening and that people wanted to know why not.

....

8) People who talk soppy to their dogs almost always do it in public as well as in private. As a vet's wife I'd noticed that. But Martin did it in private, and adopted a brisk, no-nonsense approach in public. It just didn't make sense.

a) do it ....

b) that ....

c) did it ....

d) It ....

9) You're the one who asked me to help. I can't do that if you lie to me.

....

10) If you do decide to buy, you should not do so through one person but through several, your agent, your banker, and a couple of stockbrokers.

....

11) The poorer patients paid cash when money was available, and if not, asked that the fee be charged to their account. More often than not this resulted in the fee never being paid at all.

a) if not ....

b) this ....

Finally, here is an example of 'do so' used loosely. Can you rewrite it more grammatically?

12) Andrew did not feel that they were expecting to be offered a drink, so he did not <u>do so</u>.

....

Exercise 10 (Chapter 5)

Explain what the underlined words refer to. The first one has been done for you.

0) The old greed for power? <u>It</u> is one, if not the most important, source of wars, conflicts, and family quarrels, more than <u>any other</u>, come to think of it.
   a) it = *the old greed for power*
   b) any other = *any other source of wars, conflicts, and family quarrels*

1) 'Is there anything the matter with my sisters? Is that why you're phoning?' The voice sounded anxious, less aggressive. 'To the best of my belief there's nothing the matter with <u>either of them</u>,' Andrew replied.

....

2) There was a great deal of talk about the restoration needed after the storm. The damage had not been so very great but, as in <u>all such cases</u>, more work was going to be required than I had at first thought.

....

3) Truth was truth. When in doubt tell <u>it</u>. His confession looked terrible on paper. He screwed up his first three efforts after only a line or <u>two</u>, decided that <u>the fourth</u> was as bad as <u>the others</u>, bu that <u>it</u> had to stand. He had to give them the full story. Explain to them how <u>it</u> happened.
   a) (tell) it ....
   b) two ....

c) the fourth ....
d) the others ....
e) it (had to stand) ....
f) it (happened) ....

4) If one member of staff can do so much damage any visitor, nurse, doctor or consultant, could do likewise.

....

5) Another point to remember when planning a diet is that it is not always necessary to cut a type of food out completely, but simply to replace it with something similar but more suitable, carob powder instead of chocolate for example.

....

6) This interest in preventive medicine has taken many years to develop, but at last government money is becoming available for further research. The same cannot be said to be true for research into the effects of chemical residues in food.

....

7) After 'The Shetland Bus' I wrote two novels. One was a thriller. Both are forgotten now, and deserve it. But they taught me I was not about to make my fortune as a novelist.
a) Both ....
b) it ....
c) they ....

8) But, he claimed, 'the public increasingly question the utility of institutions like the House of Lords, the judiciary, and the honours system. These institutions depend powerfully on deference, and obfuscation. Neither is compatible with a fully functioning democracy.'

....

9) Anthony loved the place and, in his will, John had made over to him most of the land, but he doubted if his son would ever live in

the house. He certainly would not do so alone. This house needed children, women, voices, confusion. Still it might happen. Anthony might yet settle down.

a) him ....

b) he ....

c) his son ....

d) do so..

e) it ....

Exercise 11 (Chapter 6)

Explain what the underlined nouns refer to.

1) The line of people waiting to be questioned pressed forward, as if by this action they could hasten the process.

   a) this action ....

   b) the process ....

2) People who organize their own disappearance may believe themselves to be acting rationally. Often the operation has been thoroughly planned and deep psychological problems that prompt such actions are well hidden.

   a) the operation ....

   b) such actions ....

3) As you release your breath, let your left leg hang further so as to stretch your stomach muscles. The same procedure should be repeated on the other leg three or four times. This action will help to strengthen the muscles.

   a) the same procedure ....

   b) this action ....

4) It is very likely indeed that the child will pretend that his homework doesn't have to be handed in for ages, and that he needn't do it until next week. The chances are that he will be saying this because he wants to watch a favourite TV

programme, so look out for the situation.

....

5) 'Ingrid appears in public, maybe has her meals in the hotel dining-room. That way we make them think her sister is still here in Stockholm. But she is not.' He cleared his throat and I guessed he was about to raise an awkward subject. 'But are we sure we can trust Ingrid?'
   a) That way ....
   b) an awkward subject ....

6) Environmental opposition delayed procedures for acquiring land, which forced the railway authority to put large stretches of new line into tunnels. This in turn caused another problem. Entering a tunnel at high speed creates pressure pulses that cause unpleasant sensations in passengers' ears.
   a) another problem ....
   b) And what was the first problem? ....

7) At the time the realization that his best friend had murdered three people didn't seem to bother Wolfe, but since then I had come to see that the whole business had really shaken him.

....

8) What we have here is a very neatly organized basic textbook for first-year mathematics students. If our students knew all of this stuff when they arrived, or even when they left, to be honest, I would be more than happy.

....

9) Mrs Williams was reading a magazine. Diana was busy talking to Stephen about something. The children were playing quietly in a corner. 'A dreadful thing has happened,' said Sophie as soon as she was sure they could not be heard. 'Your brother, my brother, I mean dear Philip, of course, has run away from school and declares he will go to sea with you.'

....

10) Another theory could be that the wounds had been inflicted afte death. There wouldn't have been much bleeding in that case. I wondered how carefully the doctor had examined the body.

....

Exercise 12 (Chapter 6)

In each of the following pieces of text, choose the best word from among the underlined alternatives, and say what it refers to.

1) Even today, when it has been widely filmed and photographed, Tibetan-style debating remains an astonishing spectacle, with i stamping, posturing and hand-clapping. No outsider since Desideri had regularly taken part in this act/action/activity.

....

2) If something won't go right in a painting, the solution is to retur to the original subject and try to see with greater clarity what you are aiming to recreate in paint. Sometimes in these circumstances / this context / this position / this experience it can be helpful to put down your brushes and make a separate drawing of the subject.

....

3) Inform air-traffic control that your aircraft has been taken over by terrorists and that you are changing course and proceeding t Cyprus. When you have done that, tell the passengers of this development/effect/result and warn them not to make any stupid moves.

....

4) Of course he'd been talking in his sleep and of course he'd not known what he was saying. But the fact that he'd said that name meant it must be in mind. Sometimes, when she reached this point, she was able to dismiss the whole episode/event/ happening as nonsense.

....

5) Hyperventilation, or overbreathing, is breathing in a rapid, shallow way using the upper chest instead of the abdomen. Breathing in this manner/method/means produces more oxygen than the body needs.

....

6) Pressure to get tough on international fossil thieves has grown steadily, along with the prices collectors pay for top-grade specimens. The fact/issue/topic has come to a head over a piece of moon rock now in the hands of a private collector in the US.

....

7) 'Here's what to do. If the police ask you, just say you can't remember who bought you the drink. Say the place was full of rich tourists and it must have been one of them.' This plan/theory/view seemed to please the boy, who grinned and said 'Right. No problem.'

....

8) Suppose you do have one hundred people who do like and approve of you. Are you happy? No, because you are worried that the one hundred and first person might not like you. This argument/belief/criticism condemns you to never being able to enjoy the positive feelings of those who do like you fully.

....

9) I am sure that there is some way in which a couple who have been turned down for adoption can be given an adult explanation for the denial/excuse/refusal.

....

10) I am going to help your parents get you better. We won't let you get any more ill, nor let you die, and nor will we let you get overweight, which I know is another doubt/fear/objection you have.

....

Exercise 13 (Chapter 8)

Rewrite the following, using a sentence adjunct to replace the words underlined. Make any other minor changes that are necessary. Note that in Examples 4 and 10 you will need a completely different word or phrase. The first one has been done for you.

0) I am being serious when I say that we'd be enormously grateful if you'd stay till we get back.
Seriously, we'd be enormously grateful if you'd stay till we get back.

1) And she knew that, if she was realistic about it, no edition of the paper could be put together, printed, and distributed the same day if the news came later than 3.45.
....

2) We are lucky that there are some clear fingerprints on the knife.
....

3) It is obvious that politics is becoming an increasingly dangerous game.
....

4) They may be mad, but – you must agree, don't you? – they don't want to starve.
....

5) It appears he's been prescribed some kind of pills, and we're supposed to make sure he doesn't drink.
....

6) Truman's performance during what you could argue was the most crucial week of his presidency was of a very high quality.
....

7) If he sued and won he would – there's no doubt about it – be awarded a very large sum of money indeed.

....

8) It is interesting to note that the things some of us find frightening, other people experience as exciting.

....

9) It was very sensible of you to decline to listen to this improper and insulting stuff.

....

0) You've got to remember that a microphone was put under my nose immediately I got off the horse. Of course when I think about it now, I would rather have not spoken on television.

....

inking words in longer texts

o far this book has shown how linking words and other reference items vork across two or three sentences. But in fact these words and phrases lso work across paragraphs, to make a longer text into a cohesive vhole. Exercises 14, 15, and 16 are designed to give you practice in using nd interpreting linking words in texts of this kind. Exercises 14 and 15 re based on written texts, while Exercise 16 uses a radio phone-in onversation to illustrate many of the words and phrases discussed in hapter 7, which are characteristic of spoken English.

'o give you additional help, an example of a longer written text is ncluded below, with comments on the use of linking and referring tems. Exercise 16 also provides comments on some of the words and hrases used, before going on to the exercise proper.

Iere is a newspaper report from *The Daily Telegraph* (August 20th, 995), about the possible existence of aliens on other planets, and about he mysterious Unidentified Flying Objects (UFOs) which some people eport seeing. The different linking and referring items are underlined, nd notes follow. The paragraphs have been numbered for ease of eference.

CLOSE ENCOUNTERS AND CONSPIRACY OF SILENCE

1 Many scientists are perfectly happy with the idea that aliens exist in our galaxy. But ask them if those same aliens have visited the Earth, and the question will be met with howls of derision.

2 The cartoon image of the Unidentified Flying Object debate has led to the emergence of a 'politically correct' stance on the issue, adopted by virtually all scientists: UFOs are definitely not alien spaceships.

3 Few will risk their scientific reputations by publicly discussing the thousand of reports that flood in every year from apparently sane members of the public

4 However, many privately admit that the standard of the UFO debate is little better than a bar-room slanging match, with 'scientific' arguments against UFOs as fatuous as claims for them.

5 Standard put-downs include claiming that aliens would have better uses fo the huge amounts of energy needed to cross interstellar space, and that – ever travelling at the speed of light – it would take thousands of years to cross the galaxy. Both arguments presume to know the motivations and the technical and physical abilities of any supposed aliens.

6 Other sceptics insist that aliens would have no reason to visit the Earth, an argument which ignores the somewhat disturbing fact that for the last 70 years radio transmissions announcing our existence have been streaming out from our planet into space – and have passed through hundreds of star systems on the way.

7 So what is the knock-out scientific argument that proves aliens have not visited us? 'There isn't one. The fact is, we just don't know,' says Professor Freeman Dyson, the distinguished British theoretical physicist at the Institute o dvanced Study at Princeton, New Jersey – and one of the few scientists happy to speak openly.

8 His reason for not investigating UFO reports is far more down to Earth. 'It's a terrible waste of time – a subject full of interesting stories that one can never check.'

Comments

Paragraph 1: 'them' = many scientists; 'those same aliens' = aliens wh exist in our galaxy; 'the question' refers back to a whole clause – th reported question 'if those same aliens have visited the Earth.'

Paragraph 2: 'a politically correct stance' refers forwards – th scientists' agreed position is that UFOs are not alien spaceships; 'th issue' = the Unidentified Flying Object debate, i.e. the debate as t whether UFOs exist, and if so what they are.

Paragraph 3: 'few' = few scientists.

Paragraph 4: 'however' is used here because there is a contrast wit the statement made in Paragraph 3; 'many' = many scientist contrasting with 'few' in Paragraph 3; 'privately' contrasts wit 'publicly' in Paragraph 3; 'them' = UFOs.

'aragraph 5: 'it' is a dummy 'it' referring forwards to the infinitive tructure 'to cross the galaxy'; 'both arguments' refers back to the two ›ut-downs' (i.e. critical remarks) mentioned, namely, that aliens ›ould have better uses for their energy than visiting the Earth, and hat it would take them thousands of years to reach us.

'aragraph 6: 'other sceptics' = other people who doubt whether UFOs re alien spaceships – the word 'sceptic' has not been used before, but ›ther' is a referring word, and it takes us back to the people behind the tandard put-downs' of Paragraph 5; 'an argument' = that aliens would ave no reason to visit the Earth.

'aragraph 7: 'so' here indicates a sort of summing up, some result from ›hat has been said so far; in this case it introduces a final question – ›hat is the knockout argument, the argument that would completely estroy the case for UFOs? – to which the answer is 'There isn't one' one' = a knockout argument).

'aragraph 8: 'his' refers to the Professor in Paragraph 7; 'it' = nvestigating UFO reports; 'a subject' refers somewhat vaguely to IFOs and whether they exist.

:xercise 14

ill each of the numbered spaces in the text with one suitable word. Cataracts are cloudy areas that form on someone's eyes, seriously ffecting their sight.)

ı addition to cataracts, Tommy Sopwith was suffering from ı)......................... eye complications, and he went into hospital full of ope (2)......................... following an operation his sight would at 3)......................... be partially restored. But, (4)........................., the peration was unsuccessful, and (5)......................... was probably the reatest regret of his life. According to his son: 'The only time I ever 5)......................... saw him knocked sideways was in hospital 7)......................... At the age of 96, Sir Thomas's sight was confined to hapes and devoid of all detail, then in the following year, 3)......................... got steadily worse, until he was unable even to tell 9)......................... a photographer had used his flashgun. Sir Thomas ever (10)......................... came to terms with his blindness.

Even in his late nineties, people still wanted to interview Sir Thomas. (11) .... his sight had gone and he was rather dea (12)........................ that was less of a problem thanks to son particularly good hearing aids. To those (13)........................ did not knc him, (14)........................ interviews could be a little disconcertin (15)........................ a question could be followed by a long silenc (16)........................ the interviewer wondered (17)........................ S Thomas had heard (18)........................ was being asked. (19)........................ he usually had heard, but was determined to factual and a suitable answer was being prepared in his mind. It was part of the Sopwith character to think (20)........................ he spoke.

Exercise 15

This exercise is adapted from a news item in *The Daily Telegra* (August 23rd, 1995). The paragraphs have been put in the wrong orde Can you use the various linking clues to put them back in the order which they originally appeared? The paragraphs have been numbere To help you, the last paragraph has been left in its correct position.

WAR CRIMES NOVELIST HAS FANTASY LIFE

1 The novel provoked public vilification and death threats because it w suspected of following the extremist line of the far right.

2 What is embarrassing to the Miles Franklin Award judges is that her book w hailed for its interpretation of 'oral history'.

3 Jill Kitson, one of the judges, said: 'The author's background is not what t judging of a literary prize is all about.'

4 She claimed that the book was a fictional account of her father's experienc in the camp. In interviews she has said most of his family was killed Communist Party officials.

5 The writer won this year's prestigious Miles Franklin Award for her first no 'The Hand that Signed the Paper', which tells of a Ukrainian's role in war crim at Treblinka concentration camp.

6 But Thomas Keneally, author of 'Schindler's Ark', said the hoax left her op to charges of making fascist propaganda.

7 But Miss Darville's reason for the hoax is a mystery.

8 Australia's literary world is in turmoil over disclosures that Helen Demiden a 24-year-old novelist, is herself a work of fiction.

9 But she is in fact the daughter of Harry and Grace Darville, who migrated fr the north of England to Brisbane before she was born.

10 Her mother said: 'It's fiction, for heaven's sake. She wrote under a pseu nym. Lots of authors do that.'

Exercise 16 (Chapter 7)

Here is part of a conversation that took place on a radio phone-in programme. The two speakers are indicated by the letters H and C. H is the presenter, or 'host' of the programme, and C is a 'caller', an ordinary member of the public. They are discussing the problem of drinking and driving. The initial greetings and introductions have already taken place, and now the conversation continues, with the caller speaking first.

First, read the whole dialogue and work through the comments that immediately follow. The underlined words and phrases are referred to in the comments or the exercise proper. Line numbers are given for ease of reference.

C: Erm, there's a lot of mention day after day and er, quite reasonably of course, it's about drink and drive.

H: Mhm.

C: Now this drink and drive thing, er it concerns a lot of people and it certainly does me because I like to have a little drink, but I never know whether I'm over the limit or under. Now some people will say 'Well you can always solve that by not drinking at all'...

H: Yeah.

C: ...but I like a drink. Now why hasn't something been invented er which is a reasonable cost, that people could buy so they could judge for themselves just as a test before they go out. If you're over the limit you leave the car in the garage, right?

H: Well those ... er those things have been invented, to be honest, and they have been on the market and the police and I are very much against them because they actually encourage people to drink don't they?

C: Erm well, there's two ways of looking at that. It doesn't encourage people to drink. Oh well, I don't think it encourages people to drink.

H: Yes it does, it encourages people to drink up to the limit. They have a drink and look at the thing and say 'Oh I'm all right I can have another one,' and I think that's a ... that's a dangerous precedent, to be honest. I think you're much better having, I mean, you know what you're supposed to have, you know, just a couple of halves or something like that erm and ...

C: No I'm not ... I'm not quite sure that I've seen these things. Now I like ...

H: I mean the ...

C: I like a drink of sherry.

H: Yeah.

C: Now I'm not sure. I ... I drink the cheapest sherry you know, er I've got a litre for about two pounds fifty at the moment on ...

H: Yeah.
C: ... on special offer. Now I can have some of that and I feel quite all right but ...
H: You might feel all right.
C: ...but er I should have gone out to a meeting tonight.
H: Yeah.
C: But I didn't go because I felt... well I'd had some drinks, I don't know how I'm fixed ...
H: Mhm.
C: ... and I can't afford to lose my licence. Now it'd be very reassuring to me if I knew er just what effect this or drink of any sort has on me.
H: Well, I mean, I still think that the people who say if you're worried about that don't drink at all are the right ones.
C: But personally I like the idea of these gadgets.
H: Well, they are available, they are on the market.
C: Are they?
H: Yes, they've been around for a year or two now but as I say the police don't like them at all, and I ... and I think I support the police fully on this.
C: But it could mean you could er have a drink now and then and not worry about losing your licence.
H: Well, I mean, the thing is you know, if you want to drink don't drive, er that's your choice isn't it really.

Comments

The numbers refer to the line numbers shown in the margin of the te

1, 4, 28, 61, etc: 'Erm' and 'er' are simply hesitation noises. Notice th they are made not only by the caller but also by the radio host, who is professional broadcaster, who might be expected to speak mo fluently.

1–2: C's first remark is very loosely constructed: tidied up it might re 'There's a lot of talk day after day – quite reasonably – about drinki and driving.'

3: H's first intervention is a mere 'mhm', perhaps showing that accepts drinking and driving as a suitable topic for discussion on t programme.

9: 'Yeah' suggests that H agrees with C's previous remark (7-8) – th the solution is not to drink. H also probably feels it is necessary to s something – even though C has not finished speaking.

10: 'Now' indicates a new (though related) topic.

14: By saying 'right', C is seeking H's agreement.

5: 'Well' indicates that H is going to give some new information. He ıen repeats himself ('those ... er those things') while thinking what to ay. This may partly be because long silences are unacceptable on a adio programme, where the listeners cannot see the speakers.

)–20: C uses 'erm well' to introduce his disagreement politely; he does ot think that this alcohol-testing gadget would encourage drinking. ut 'oh well' softens his disagreement – he's saying that he is xpressing a personal opinion.

4–26: H twice says 'I think'. This phrase can stress that it is only a ersonal opinion, but it may be a strongly held opinion.

6–27: 'I mean' adds emphasis here to what follows – 'you know what ou're supposed to have', i.e. everyone knows the amount of alcohol ıat is supposed to be safe. (This first 'you know' is not a fluency filler.)

7: The second 'you know' is a fluency filler, though not meaningless. It nplies that C must also know that the recommended amount of drink 'a couple of halves', i.e. no more than two half pints of beer.

1: H is trying to make a point here ('I mean the') but he has ıterrupted C, causing C to repeat 'I like' (30, 32) before continuing his emark.

ow read the whole text through again, and look at the questions on ıe later part. In each case, say which you think is the most likely nswer. Again, numbers refer to line numbers.

C says 'I drink the cheapest sherry <u>you know</u>' (34–35) because
a) he has already told H this
b) he expects H to know about cheap sherry
c) he is checking that H is listening

When H says 'yeah' (37), he
a) agrees that cheap sherry costs two pounds fifty
b) interrupts because he knows what C is going to say
c) wants to show he is still in the conversation

In '<u>Now</u> I can have some of that ...' (38), 'now' implies
a) C is introducing new information
b) in the past, C could not drink sherry and still feel all right
c) he can only drink sherry because it is cheap

4) C says 'well' (43) because
   a) he is starting his remark again
   b) he means 'as well', another way of saying 'also'
   c) he is showing surprise

5) When H says 'mhm' (45) he means that he
   a) doubts what C says
   b) is thinking what to say next
   c) is listening

6) 'Well, I mean, I still think' (49): The radio host
   a) wants to change the topic
   b) is gently re-stating his disagreement with what C is saying
   c) is sympathizing with C's wish to drink

7) 'As I say' (55-56): The radio host
   a) is changing the subject
   b) is emphasizing what he has already said
   c) is using a fluency filler to give himself time to think

8) 'The thing is' (60): The host
   a) is stating his opinion firmly, in the hope of bringing t conversation to a close
   b) is changing his opinion on drink-driving
   c) is suggesting C is free to choose to drink and drive

Answer Key

Exercise 1

1) The sandwich made him feel better, both because he had been hungry and because for a while he could pretend that this was just a normal day.
2) ... It both opened a door and kept it locked.
3) He doesn't look like either his uncle or his aunt.
4) No one would either know or care what became of them.
5) You either got the order or you didn't.
6) Her nails were neither long nor painted.
7) She neither wept nor despaired.
8) Neither Anthony nor Fred was a skilled mechanic.
9) ...his head, he not only felt the pain of the bruise but also heard the crinkle...
10) Not only did she pay him a top salary, but the job kept him moving and happy.
11) He would be made familiar with the layout of Geneva, not only from maps but also from a large-scale model.
12) If the river carried the body down, then (it follows that) this is where the body entered the water.
13) If land was nearby, then they might be able to obtain fuel...
14) If this view is right, then (that would mean) perhaps we have been applying the wrong tests...

Exercise 2

1) If he had not unfortunately been tone deaf, he might have made a fortune as a singer.
2) Tibetan was to be taught during the three years of primary school. However, all secondary education...
3) (You must) prune these trees. Otherwise, you won't get any fruit off them.
4) Elsie poured out tea and they all drank a cup. Soon afterwards Aunt Mamie announced...
5) While they were living at the house with...a shared nanny, the war grew closer and bombs began to fall...
6) I moved the chair back from the doorway so that I could be seen from the outer office but not overheard.
7) ...I used it for about two to three years, generously applying it every morning, so that my skin is now quite thin on my face.
8) ...'I suppose I shall, provided that the police don't want me to stay here.'
9) Ireland worked as a team with clever passing among the forwards. By contrast, England relied on individual efforts.
10) Unemployment seems to have contributed to increasing crime rates. However, this has not generally resulted in more people being sent to prison...
11) He had enjoyed the lively company of his friends in Edinburgh. All the same, his work, he felt, demanded solitude.
12) Some UN sources expressed hope that a deal would be struck. The Americans, on the other hand, were less optimistic.
13) Despite the fact that they knew OR Despite knowing it was wrong..., most of those interviewed...did not consider themselves criminals.
14) ... 'There's an important murder trial going on and I'm the main police witness. Still, it won't matter a lot'.
15) ... Meanwhile Patrick and Margaret talked quietly.
16) We had a wonderful time there, except that we had our money stolen on the last day.

Exercise 3

1) a) By contrast
   b) on the contrary
   c) on the contrary
2) a) though OR although
   b) though
   c) though
3) a) no matter
   b) no matter
   c) for that matter
4) a) in case
   b) in case
   c) In any case
5) a) Granted
   b) Given that
   c) given (that)
6) a) All the same
   b) at the same time
   c) all the same
7) a) above all
   b) above all
   c) After all
8) a) in the meantime (OR meanwhile)
   b) Meanwhile
   c) in the meantime (OR meanwhile)

Exercise 4

1) from the time when
2) because
3) the whole time that
4) provided that
5) in order that
6) with the result that
7) more or less the same as
8) although...greatly
9) rather than
10) earlier than
11) although
12) whereas

Exercise 5

1) for
2) yet
3) in case
4) even though
5) so
6) lest
7) as though
8) wherever
9) until
10) on condition that

Exercise 6

1) Nevertheless
2) however
3) instead
4) Alternatively
5) Accordingly
6) At least
7) therefore
8) Hence
9) So
10) anyway
11) Moreover
12) indeed
13) namely
14) Next
15) Likewise

Exercise 7

1) Whatever I do will be well thought out.
2) It suddenly dawned on me (that) it must be Pete's brother.
3) We don't know what we are looking for.
4) We are certain (that) this man is your brother.
5) He felt he was closer than he had been before to whatever was going on in the investigation.
6) The vital factor was that improved breathing would bring better co-ordination.
7) It's beyond me why they should wish to look like that appalling man.
8) You can't run away from the fact that we have 28 professionals.
9) From the contents it is clear that the document has been wrongly dated and ought to read 1932 instead of 1931.
10) Whoever said history repeats itself first as tragedy, then as farce, was right.
11) Please listen carefully to what I say OR what I am going to say.
12) They are still arguing over who it belongs to.
13) It doesn't matter whose money it is.
14) Let's talk about how we should handle this.

Exercise 8

1) After leaving the hotel early in the morning, he headed for the public library, taking up his usual position . . .
2) He grew impatient if told that something could not be done . . .
3) He stared vacantly at the people milling around as if unaware of the commotion.
4) . . . they would need a week before taking action.
5) Even when asked a direct question, she scarcely bothered to answer.
6) . . . they would still be expensive, especially if available to all.
7) He poured himself another drink, unwilling to lose the moment and the memory.
8) I've heard that Joe Wilson, though unwilling to part with any money during his life, would leave everything to her after his death.
9) Do you think that while still in motion his cycle was kicked from behind?
10) How do we choose? Having chosen, how do we know that this is the best choice?
11) Without realizing it, she was moving along the road, unaware of its crystal-hard covering of ice.
12) Realizing that she was blocking his path, she stepped cautiously to one side.
13) Although unhappy with the opinion polls, Republicans argued yesterday that they would receive a boost . . .
14) He finished the tea and laid the cup aside, not expecting her to answer.
15) Mother had had a fainting fit on hearing the news.
16) The doctors have been marvellous in explaining everything.
17) Joanna startled Enid by giving her an utterly inappropriate hug.
18) (With) his eyes fixed on the lake, he made the sort of meaningless remarks that the occasion required.

Exercise 9

1) (to extend a hand,) to touch the body lying there
2) if they don't arrive before I leave
3) for drivers to leave the highway here
4) a) nightmares
   b) terrible, hideous, frightening
5) a) (go to) a local hospital in Sussex
   b) advising a local hospital in Sussex
   c) hospital
   d) to be in the country and not too far from home
6) a) that we have any valuables anywhere else in the house that need checking
   b) giving our son a great many things when he married
7) why nothing was happening
8) a) talk soppy to their dogs
   b) that people who talk soppy to their dogs

almost always do it in public as well as in private
c) talked soppy to his dog
d) the fact that Martin talked soppy to his dog in private, and adopted a brisk, no-nonsense approach in public
9) help
10) buy
11) a) if money was not available
b) (the poorer patients) asking that the fee be charged to their account
12) 'Do so' is a substitution item, and the intended meaning is 'offer them a drink', but this phrase does not appear in the sentence as it stands. The writer could have written 'Andrew did not feel that they were expecting him to offer them a drink.'

Exercise 10

1) either of your sisters
2) all cases of restoration needed after a storm
3) a) the truth
b) two lines
c) the fourth effort
d) the other efforts
e) the fourth effort
f) the incident or episode he is confessing
4) do a similar amount of damage too
5) some food similar to the food you are cutting out
6) that government money is becoming available
7) a) the two novels I wrote after 'The Shetland Bus'
b) to be forgotten
c) the two novels I wrote after 'The Shetland Bus'
8) neither deference nor obfuscation
9) a) Anthony
b) John
c) John's son, Anthony
d) live in the house
e) Anthony might settle down and live in the house (perhaps with a wife, children, etc)

Exercise 11

1) a) pressing forward
b) the process of being questioned
2) a) the action of organizing one's own disappearance
b) acts of organizing one's own disappearance
3) a) letting your leg hang further so as to stretch your stomach muscles
b) letting your leg hang further and repeating the procedure
4) the situation in which a child pretends that his homework is not urgent because he wants to watch television
5) a) because Ingrid is seen to appear in public, maybe having her meals in the hotel dining-room
b) the question of whether or not we can trust Ingrid
6) a) pressure pulses that cause unpleasant sensations in passengers' ears, when trains enter a tunnel at high speed.
b) the requirement to put large stretches of new line into tunnels, made necessary by environmental opposition
7) the fact that his best friend had murdered three people
8) the information in the basic mathematics textbook
9) the fact that Philip has run away from school and says he wants to go to sea with his brother
10) if the wounds had been inflicted after death

Exercise 12

1) activity = Tibetan-style debating
2) these circumstances = when something won't go right in a painting
3) development = that the plane has been taken over by terrorists and is changing course to fly to Cyprus
4) episode = the man talking in his sleep and saying that particular name
5) manner = a rapid, shallow way, using the upper chest instead of the abdomen
6) issue = the problem of what to do about international fossil theft
7) plan = the suggestion that the boy should say he couldn't remember who bought him the drink, probably a rich tourist
8) belief = that the one hundred and first person might not like you
9) refusal = the authorities refusing to allow a couple to adopt a child
10) fear = that you will get overweight

Exercise 13

1) And she knew that, realistically, no edition of the paper could be put together...
2) Luckily (for us), there are some clear fingerprints...
3) Obviously, politics is becoming an increasingly dangerous game.
4) They may be mad, but surely they don't want to starve.
5) Apparently he's been prescribed some kind of pills...
6) ...during what was arguably the most crucial week... (OR ...during what arguably

was the most crucial week...)

7) ...he would undoubtedly be awarded a very large sum... OR ...he would without (any) doubt be awarded a very large sum...
8) Interestingly, the things some of us find frightening...
9) You very sensibly declined to listen to this improper and insulting stuff.
10) ... Of course, on reflection (OR with hindsight), I would rather have not spoken on television.

Exercise 14

The words used in the original text are given first, with other acceptable words in brackets.

1) other
2) that
3) least
4) unfortunately (sadly, alas)
5) this
6) really
7) afterwards
8) it
9) when (if, whether)
10) really
11) then
12) although (but)
13) who (that)
14) such (these)
15) because (as, since)
16) while
17) if (whether)
18) what
19) fact
20) before

Exercise 15

The original order of the paragraphs was 8, 5, 4, 9, 2, 3, 6, 1, 7, 10.

Exercise 16

1) b
2) c
3) a
4) a
5) c
6) b
7) b
8) a

Index

References are to paragraph numbers, not pages. Lexical items (words and phrases) discussed in the text are shown in **bold** type. Topics, categories of words, and grammatical terms are shown in ordinary type, or in ***bold italic*** if they are referred to in the Glossary (pp. vii–x).